All Ground Up

Phillip Finkelstein

Dedicated to all those who made it through Covid and to their loved ones who did not.

Main Characters

1. Steve- Husband of Ann, hiker and writer.

2. Ann- Fulltime Bubbe (Grandma).

3. Theo- Mayor of Western Avenue. Also a philosopher.

4. Russ- Manager of Cera's Grocery Store and all-around good guy.

5. Parking Paul- Thinker and squirrel expert.

6. Beatrice- Retired cop and painter.

7. Rick- Late blooming historian.

8. Ted- Irish pipefitter and sculptor.

9. Tim- Real estate developer and certified car nut.

10. Stu- Day trader and best friend of Tim.

11. Fred- The General. Rim rod World War Two Vet.

12. Ralph- Retired chemistry teacher and tango dancer.

Table of Contents

Poem: Covid Time, Covid Shine ix

Prologue: xi

Chapters:

1. The Return 1
2. How People Got By 19
3. We All Had Losses, Some Remain Lost. 35
4. Indian Boundary Park 40
5. The Mostly Cooperative Life 44
6. Ann and Steve 49
7. Anne and Steve Make a Run for it 54
8. Back Where They Sort of Belong. 60
9. Still Being Cooperative. 85
10. The Losses Continue. 89
11. A Death. 94
12. The Next Day 100
13. The New Semi- Normal. 111
14. Just Walk Away. 125
15. Meet Up to Break up. 130
16. Simple Courage of Everyday Life. 132
17. Coffee Sometimes Falls Flat. 134
18. Burnt Toast Lodge 137
19. The Neighs Have it. 145
20. The Best Hike is the Current Hike. 152
21. The Dream Team 163
22. Steve and Ann for the Ages. 184
23. You can always find it at Cera's 188
24. Another Cup of Coffee 194
25. Party On! 200
26. Final Cup of Coffee 205
27. Steve and Kayla 213

Epilog Looking Back -How we made through Covid. (Sort of) 225

Timeline-The Lost Years or The Years That Weren't. 231

Covid Time, Covid Shine

It was a time

When we lived

Holding our breath.

Not knowing when or how

Or even if

We,

Our beloved children

Our beloved children's children

Would make it to another day.

You could almost

Smell the Fear.

Holding each other's hand.

Saying, almost praying

We all (Thank God) were still here.

Those of us remaining

Watched the sun rise.

Yet again

and waited to see if it was hopefully

Not beyond our expiration date.

Pf 12-30-22

Prologue:

It was a clear day, but Lake Michigan was enraged. Waves came in like angry fists. These were not gentle waves massaging the shore. Instead, they broke on the rocks, piers and anything else that was unlucky enough to be located by the lake. Only the lake foam was left to answer why the water was so powerful. Steve watched for a minute, trying to understand what had happened to them all and why. But he wasn't going to get any answers from the lake today. He usually didn't, so after a long minute, he turned and walked away.

But Covid didn't. January of 2020 started with vague rumors of some new pandemic that was sweeping through China and might threaten the world. At first, like most people, Steve wasn't worried. Heck, they lived in the most advanced country with the best medical services in the world. They had local, state and federal health agencies looking out for them and besides, there must be a pill or a plan to stop it from spreading to the US. But there wasn't a plan that was out there at first. Instead, Covid spread like a biblical plague, killing first, tens of thousands, then hundreds of thousands. By 2022, it had killed over one million Americans alone. People died so quickly that it overwhelmed the hospitals. Cold, dead people had to be placed in storage because funeral homes could not keep up with the volume. People died in isolation without family, because of necessary quarantines. It was a tough and ugly way to die: alone.

Even survivors had a difficult time acknowledging their new hellish world. People had to socially distance to avoid being infected. With masks on, people did not recognize longtime friends or neighbors, even when they felt brave enough or desperate enough to leave their isolation chambers i.e. homes. It was a dark ugly world, and the gloom was slow to dissipate even after the Covid Vaccines became more readily available. It was a cold hard time, no matter what the temperature read.

1. The Return.

Theo was up early, it wasn't even 3:00 AM, but it was a big day, an important day. The Coffee Klatch was meeting at a new location at Cera's Grocery on Ridge. Guys had given up on McDonald's restaurant on Western Avenue. Dealing with Crazy Larry had gotten to be too much with his constant panhandling and shrieking to himself. Theo was sympathetic, after all, Larry was someone's father or brother. But enough was enough. So, the coffee club did what guys generally do when faced with a difficult problem- they tried to avoid it by moving on. And like most problems, Larry would eventually find his way back to them.

Good grief though, it was not an easy process of deciding where to meet next. Especially with this group of rotating characters. Like any self-administrated coffee group, people drifted in and out as their moods and needs necessitated. That's why they needed a consistent location. Otherwise, where would people go to be entertained, abused and generally led astray? Nate's breakfast joint was long gone, a victim of Covid and mismanagement. Steve liked the idea of the new Starbucks on Touhy Avenue, but the other guys weren't willing or able to spend

$5 for a coffee every day with no free refills. Stu wanted to try Edelstein's Deli, but they still were not offering indoor seating because of continuing Covid concerns. Joe liked House of Pancakes but who wanted to watch him order and slowly chew the same $6.99 senior special every day? Ralph, as usual, kept his preferences to himself. Conrad, Curt, Lou and Jimmy were still in Arizona. Joe and Fred simply didn't care, figuring this would give them superseding kvetching rights. Dunkin Donuts on Howard was an option, but parking was tight and who knew how long they would be open.

No question, times were tough- especially for restaurants. Covid had been the toughest grey cloud that people couldn't seem to escape. If it didn't kill you or your business, it still battered your spirit. For others, it left their minds in a permanent fog, making it difficult to make decisions. After watching his friends bicker for a week, Theo finally made an executive decision to meet at Cera's. Making decisions was not an issue for Theo. He had run a very successful minimart gas station that the Westridge neighborhood in Chicago relied on for decades. Indeed, Theo was still referred to as the Mayor of Western Avenue because he knew everyone and greeted every single person he came in contact with as a potential voter. He bragged that he had never traveled north of Howard Avenue and lived his whole life in Westridge. Retired for over 13 years, Theo still made daily rounds in his 2011 Kia. So, after making rounds driving Western from Peterson to Howard then Kedzie to Devon, Theo drove to Cera's Grocery. Deciding to meet at Cera's was not a difficult decision. Cera's had an expansive seating area that was never crowded at 7 am, and Russ the store manager agreed to make coffee for a buck a piece with free refills. Russ was good that way. Besides, Russ and Theo went back a long time. Way back.

Russ was already busy making coffee in a large stainless-steel urn. Russ was a thin guy with brillo colored hair in his early 40's. He had gotten married in his late thirties and between work and 3-year-old twins, he put on 25,000 to 30,000 steps a day. It wasn't unusual for Russ to walk 30 miles a week at work. Russ thought he should be able to get a tax deduction for the sneakers he wore to work. He had to replace them every 2 or 3 months.

"Thought you deserved fresh and not 2-day old coffee. Those guys in the meat department who leave it plugged in for days are really animals." Even Russ couldn't stomach it.

Those guys could drink anything, even several days-old coffee, and often did.

"You sure a buck per guy is gonna be enough?" As a business owner, Theo knew how even pennies added up.

"Yeah, we got dented coffee cans we can't use otherwise." Russ was practical. Keeping a business going during Covid, he had to be.

"Well, thanks for doing this anyways. You didn't have to…" Theo was grateful.

"Yeah, I did. You know why." Russ always paid his debts.

In Russ's final year of high school, Theo had found free lodging for Russ as a night attendant at Nemer's Mortuary, when Russ's drunk dad fled after their house was repossessed. This had been less than 2 years after Russ's mom died of breast cancer. Some guys get all the Tsuris (bad luck).

An uncomfortable silence followed, then Theo asked:

"How's Judy and the kids?"

"Doing good-all things considered." As Russ knew well, thanks to Covid, everything had to be considered.

Russ's wife, Judy, was a school nurse over at Foster Elementary. From Russ, Theo heard second hand of the difficult time Judy had navigating between parents, teachers and administration, all of whom were frantic (parents believed they were just prudent) over Covid. Theo was grateful that he was long retired and that the most difficult decision he faced, most days, was choosing between Jeopardy and Family Feud game shows on television. Parents had a much tougher gig. Making risk assessments over the health of their kids, was a daily responsibility for them. Fortunately, most parents chose or at least tried to guess right, what would be safe enough for their children? A parent never knew for sure and most worried.

Just then Parking Paul came in. Limping as usual. Parking Paul, (no one knew his last name) had retired at age 70 when his right knee decided it wasn't going to put up with the nonsense of walking 8 hours every day for work as a City Parking Enforcement Officer. So, the knee did what teenagers do when they're upset- it blew up. With that, it also blew up Paul's life. Paul had wanted to work indefinitely. Now it was definite that it wasn't gonna happen. Many a morning at the coffee club had been spent on advising Paul what to do with his life AFTER work. Some people work to live, others live to work. Problem for Paul was, the latter lifestyle choice left him in throbbing pain.

"Morning Gents, coffee, ready yet?' Paul eased himself gingerly into the booth. No use volunteering about his pain. He almost never complained about the constant aches. According to the Official Guy's Code Book, it wouldn't make a difference anyway.

"Russ is making the real stuff."

"Real coffee for real men." Several heads nodded. Still, Theo was hopeful that Beatrice would make it. Beatrice was a retired female cop who had weathered 27 years of drunks, jerks and rampant sexism when her art degree did not and could not pay off. Beatrice was short and stout. The guys joked that she truly had "broad" shoulders, appropriate for a cop in Chicago. The guys missed seeing her since she didn't show up as often anymore. That was common with Covid. People drifted in and out. Kind of like the waves of Lake Michigan.

The large screen TV was already on and spewing the news. Theo moved to turn down the volume. No use starting a political argument on their first day back at the new location. Many a friendship had been lost over a strongly held belief. People no longer belonged to political parties, they belonged to electronic tribes.

It had been only a couple months since they started getting back together. So far, so good. None had come down with a bad case of Covid, that they could tell. (Keep in mind that over 30% of the cases were asymptomatic and people didn't know they had it- let alone spreading it.)

Ralph was alone with his thoughts when he arrived. Ralph sat in the back as usual. Funny, that even Coffee Klatches had unspoken assigned seating. He was pretty quiet these days ever since he lost his mother to Covid in the nursing home in the beginning of the scourge. Like so many others, he hadn't even been able to say goodbye when she succumbed so quickly. Ralph was left only with a heavy dose of survivor's guilt that he carried quietly. Back then, a lot of people lost family that way: the soon to be departed woke up with a cold, then had great difficulty breathing. By the time they reached the hospital, it was already too late. The guys had tried to get Ralph to talk about it then, while they were still stuck zooming, but Ralph would swallow his pain and reply that there was nothing further to say. So, he didn't. But at least Ralph came to coffee. When he didn't, Theo would track him down and guilt him into attendance. Otherwise, Ralph stayed alone in his mother's home, with his memories and collection of Civil War history.

Then Tim walked in, right on time, his time, of 8:13 with his cell phone glued to his ear. He was speaking loudly, as if his increased volume would make people understand: "Because

I said so, that's why." Tim was exasperated. Most successful apartment owners were, and especially around the 5th of the month when rents were overdue. The rental business was difficult enough even before the Covid limitations: "We can't keep carrying him. This is his third time in 2 years. As soon as we can file for an eviction-we should." Tim shook his head and clicked his phone shut. Hard. When are his kids gonna learn that the owner (and he was a generous one) decided when he was giving a donation, not the tenant? Then he remembered where he was and put on his best real estate developer's smile. It did feel good to just have coffee with the guys. He expelled his frustrated landlord's lament and took a deep breath. Maybe he could just sell the real estate to his kids now? Let them deal with the daily, no hourly stress. Favorable terms of course. He could then go to coffee several times a week and work on his cars.

The rest of them were having a highly spirited discussion as to what car company had the best paint jobs in the 60's. They had this discussion many times before. Still no resolution. Probably never would be. So today instead, they moved on to a discussion of which was better: the thick rich car colors of the 60's versus the current available rust protection. Those present looked to Tim for leadership. They had to, their opinion did not necessitate knowledge. Tim was the acknowledged expert on cars. After all, he had really smart hands. Not because he owned 13 collector cars but because he was a car nut who actually worked on the cars himself. Tim even showed the cars annually at his usual spot by the Space Tower near his friend Errol at the Minnesota State Fair. Tim, a natural leader, was determined to settle this inane discussion on colors, once and for all: "Look guys, there no question that the 60's paint jobs were better. They're thicker, richer. Today's robotic paint jobs are so thin you could probably blow it off with a fart."

They all laughed, and Tim hoped they could finally move on to something else. Anything but Covid. For the most part, they had left the Pandemic discussions behind in the rearview mirror, since the vaccines came to society's rescue. Like Theo said, they just had to keep on moving forward. "What else are you going to do?" Fair point. Still, underneath the veneer of normalcy, Covid was ever present and sulked in the background, waiting for its chance to re-emerge. But for these true survivors, life moved on and so did their discussion.

Rick, who had wandered in between the differences of a 60's Pontiac versus Buick body style-he had some interesting news. At age 68, now working on a master's in history in retirement, after 30 long years of delivering pizzas and before that construction, Rick had just been appointed a teaching assistant.

"That's great. Rick. Maybe some of the students' grandmothers will be interested in dating you." Theo said it with a smile but was proud of what Rick had accomplished. They all were. Steve thought Rick's achievement was much more impressive than Steve's managing to sit still long enough to pick up a law degree in his 20's. As for the others, the lure of additional formal education in their later years, was nonexistent. They already knew what they needed to know. Now, as for firm opinions, the guys were always willing to share them, even if it hadn't been solicited or necessary. As for facts, the table believed that objective facts should never get in the way of a clear, subjective truth. It usually didn't- even with Google being a mere voice command away.

It was after all, a motley group of men mostly in their 60's and 70's. Mostly self-employed, they were looking at or had successfully passed the end of the occupational finish line. Like most guys, they had spent more time planning financially rather than emotionally, as to what their lives would be like after they stopped clocking in. So, the Coffee Klatch became an emotional lifeline, not that they would ever use such a term. Still, even when the regulars didn't show up for a while, they worried, and Theo called. They all knew they had a place where they belonged, even if it didn't come with a membership card. The free daily abuse was a bonus.

So, as a result, they all came most days in their own manner and at their own speed.

Stu was early. Usually was. Learning that was an important lesson that served Stu well. He was wearing a baseball hat. They almost all did, as if the hat would cover the loss of hair and youth, long gone bye. Stu had been a semi successful car salesman and also knew the importance of just showing up in life. He had been successful selling Cadillacs until the market changed and millennials were not interested in land yachts. Even after Stu got himself a rug for the top of his head to look younger, he still couldn't relate to the younger generations and their unecessary SUVs. So, three years ago he quit his job, ditched the hair rug and took his 2012 Cadillac SRX station wagon home to sulk. After an appropriate mourning period, Stu got back to work as a Stock Day Trader, and surprisingly did well. Like he told his wife Mary, the less Stu knew about a company, the better he did trading their stock. Mostly. There was still a significant trading loss he had tried to cover by closing a 401K account. While he hadn't told Mary yet, he was going to when the time was right. So far Stu had been waiting over 2 years for the right time. He had cut down on his day trading. As soon as Stu got back up to even, he was going to quit. This time for sure.

Joe was well-Joe. He was a successful sewer drain cleaning franchisee who was lucky enough to be bought out when the parent company went private. Joe liked to say he was "plumb lucky." That he knew when to sell his business when he did. Joe still had the strong forearms of a man who was used to wrestling steel pipe and toilets at 3 am in the morning when frantic callers found him on the web for 24-hour emergency service. He didn't miss those days and nights at all. He spent most of his free time now chasing fish at his cabin in Wisconsin. He usually wasn't successful. Most fisherman who bragged about their big catches- weren't.

Fred, in his 80's, was a force of nature. He stood 6 feet 2 inches tall and still had a military bearing, even when he sat. No wonder the guys called him, the General, but only behind his back. He had after all, served in the Navy during World War 2. While he had run the family fur store for many years, he now was a successful financial investor. But what he really invested in were people. He was the kind of guy who could measure people by their handshake, and often did.

Then, there was Ted who had immigrated from Ireland and later made his way to Chicago after 2 years of service in the U.S. Army. He liked to joke that he skipped like a small stone across the Atlantic Ocean and the Great Lakes to reach the Windy City. A silver haired man of moderate height, his wide shoulders belied the fact that he had worked union construction for 23 years before retiring to become a popular lounge singer. Married to his childhood sweetheart, Grace, Steve enjoyed the fact that Ted had played innumerable Bar Mitzvahs and Weddings.

Finally, there were the stragglers/characters who may or may not be there on a regular basis and this included Crazy Larry, and of course, Beatrice. The retired cop stopped being a regular after she moved into a home by the Leaning Tower of Pisa that was more conveniently located in Niles, Illinois. Beatrice bought the home to house her new dog which she figured correctly was cheaper than paying for therapy. Though the gourmet dog food was expensive, at least there weren't any co-pays.

Larry was the sad story of a brilliant PHD physicist gone awry, after his beloved wife Toni died. Toni had kept him on his meds and working at the Argonne National Laboratory for decades. After her death, his paranoia was unchecked and usually involved the danger of imminent nuclear war in the Middle East. An hour later, he would be fine, but the guys could only take limited doses. As a former, highly respected physicist, he did know the danger highly riled up atoms could do. Theo knew the danger of when people didn't have a place where they could talk or in the case of Larry. occasionally shriek. In any case, Theo made everyone feel welcome, even Larry who eventually figured out their new hideout. It was a rare gift.

There was never a shortage of things to talk about. If the conversation was dragging, the Chicago Sun Times newspaper was always good for cannon fodder. Literally- some numbskull would toss the paper at each other. At least twice a week, there was a highly spirited discussion of how unsafe the city was (true) and how the mayor was only making it worse. (not true according to Steve who described himself as a staunch and starched Democrat.)

They moved on to a particularly frustrating discussion of replacing Steve's bathroom wall tile which was original, and dated back to the 1920's. It was a shiny lime color. Disgusting, especially to Ann, Steve's wife. What made it especially annoying to

Steve was the fact he had erroneously brought it up in the first place. Number Three Rule of the Coffee Club was to never bring up a repair issue unless one was prepared for the others to spend his money. Ann was looking for something to improve the look of their bathroom, (read spend real money). While Steve was typically inclined to just agree (It saved time.) Steve felt her idea to paint the tile, would be no more effective than painting his liver, a rosier and healthier color. Neither would produce a long-term, satisfactory result. Already, 3 out of 3 contractors advised them to just leave the bathroom wall tile alone. They all advised that it was going to be extremely difficult to remove tile in such a small area that had so many large mirrors. After all, the tiles never did anything to them. As did the entire coffee group, Steve felt this bathroom repair attempt would be a financial and emotional disaster. Steve had already offered to remodel the whole bathroom and update it in any color Ann wanted. Ann turned it down, not being willing to go without a toilet for several weeks during the construction process. Steve didn't think he could hold out that long either. Steve suffered from clinched jaw syndrome, every time he thought about the project. Fred calmly advised him to just sell the darn place. As a military guy who had seen battle, Fred knew sometimes, you just had to accept your losses, and move forward.

But this is what the coffee klatch did most mornings- sharing the pains and gains of life. Unlike their wives, who in book clubs, thoughtfully opined on books with whine and wine, these guys grunted their thoughts with coffee. Occasionally, they might even share their feelings, usually by accident. Steve wondered if he should bring up his new diagnosis of Prostate Cancer. Nah, that could be deferred for another day. After all it was already 9 am. Fred stood up, pushed in his chair authoritatively, and effectively ended the morning session. He was good at that.

2. How People Got By.

People had left in a hurry as if they didn't want to get stuck with the restaurant tab. They all had places to go, doctors to meet. People were much more impatient since Covid. Accident rates were up. People were always in a rush. But who could blame them? It was as if they all lost several years of their lives due to the Pandemic. Perhaps, they had. And they were the lucky ones who were still on the right side of the grass. (Alive)

People applied many strategies to get through the quarantine and beyond. The use of Netflix, Zoom and Amazon exploded.

The Coffee Guys tried varying approaches to get by in the long months that quarantine and social distancing were in practice. While Steve and Ann hid from Covid in Arizona, most of the other guys remained at home where they could binge watch and snack their way through TV series and movies. A few like the residents of Park Gables gardened, while a fair number nibbled at trading stocks daily. Stu's motto remained: "sometimes you had to lose money to lose more money." It was not a profitable motto. Kind of accurate, though. The wives seemed to handle the quarantine better. They would walk the park in groups and still had a role to play in their extended families, even if they were on the outside of their children's homes looking in. Literally- due to social distancing requirements. The daily and then weekly zoom calls seemed to be a roll call of what was new with people (usually nothing} and who came down with Covid. It was depressing and many of the guys found themselves self-medicating through alcohol. A lot. Many people developed a Covid gut which was 20 to 30 extra pounds due to heavy duty snacking. Frito-Lay never had it so good.

Their friends did realize how fortunate they were for the most part compared to others. But still there was no rhyme or reason as to whose family and friends were hit by the pandemic and whose weren't. It just was what it was. The physical and emotional toll was exhausting, even to members of the Coffee Klatch.

At some point, Theo had to drive to Ralph's house on Falwell when Ralph did not show up for 2 weeks at coffee and would not return telephone calls. Ralph lived in a quaint white stucco bungalow that he shared with his mother before she died. Bungalows were all the rage in Chicago in the 1920's and 1930's and builders built thousands of them. They were practical and affordable. After all, the average Chicago Bungalow only cost $5,000 to $7500 then to build and had 1200 square feet, including a full basement.

Theo pounded on the door with authority like a cop: bam, bam, bam. Theo sounded like a Chicago Cop, too: "I know you're in there, I can see your car on the street. (It was a distinctive 1972 green Ford Torino.) Open up." Bam, bam, bam. Theo still had surprising strength in his arms in his 80's. Very impressive.

"I'm not here...Go away." That response didn't make any sense even to Ralph, whose mouth uttered it.

"Come on, this ain't right. I can't keep on stopping by every couple of months and disturbing the neighbors." Theo was getting tired of being everybody's nursemaid, especially Ralph, who seemed to need his diaper changed more often than the other guys. Then again, Ralph was all alone and didn't have anyone else.

Theo tried a different tactic: "The guys miss you. Just the other day, Rick and Ted were arguing over the Irish Race Riots of 1973. They need you to settle it."

The door opened and Ralph let him in: "That was 1863 during the Civil War." Ralph, a retired High School Chemistry teacher was a stickler about getting his facts right. An only child, Ralph was always willing to admit when he was wrong but then again, he never was.

"Whatever." The truth was, Theo didn't really care, and had made the whole thing up. He was much more interested in the three-foot pile of empty TV dinners stacked against the dining room table and multiple books on the couch. This guy needed a domestic supervisor in the worst way.

"I thought you had a cleaning person?" Theo didn't want to be too accusatory right off the bat.

"She quit when I wouldn't double her salary. She said that I was three times the work of her other clients."

Surveying the mess strewn across several rooms, Theo was inclined to agree: "You think she might have a point, Mr. Tidy-bowl?" Theo again promised himself that he would never use Ralph's bathroom, it might not be safe.

"Nope, didn't need to. I bought permanent help on sale at Kohl's Department Store on close out." Ralph beamed.

Now that he thought about it, Theo could hear a distant whirling sound in the background. At first, he thought it was his hearing aid acting up again: "What is it?"

"It's my new roommate and cleaning partner – the Jackie 2000."

Come to think of it, apart from the piles of messes, Theo thought the carpet did look pretty clean: "You gave it a name?"

Just on cue, Jackie whirled into the living room. It was a small, round, flashing robotic cleaning device-about sixteen inches wide. Ralph was defensive: "Well, of course I did. It's not an it, it's called Jackie and Jackie cleans better when I treat it right."

It made perfect sense to Ralph and perfect nonsense to Theo. He had read about when people gave human attributes to a machine. Theo thought it was called personification or machinification. Whatever. Ralph's behavior was very concerning to Theo who had tried getting Ralph into counseling before, right after his mother's death. While Theo didn't put much stock in counseling and the like for himself, he figured it might be a help to someone like Ralph who had no one to talk to. Problem was Ralph thought he had someone, Jackie, to unload his burdens to. Lots of people during and after Covid needed someone to talk to. Theo thought he would broach the topic again:

"Hey Ralph, how about we go out to lunch and then check out one of those drop-in counseling centers? My treat."

"No can do today. Jackie and I are taking Tango lessons on Netflix at 12:30. Sorry, I gotta get ready. I'll see you at coffee tomorrow." Ralph opened the front door. Theo could take a hint. Ralph at least looked happy and was at least getting some exercise. As he drove home, Theo was reminded that everyone had to try and get over Covid in their own way and in their own fashion.

Still, most humans by nature are optimistic, and that usually served them well. Americans were eager to get their lives back to what they were B.C. i.e., before Covid.

Against all odds, the country started reopening again in the spring of 2020. The vaccines were still being developed. Despite over 100,000 deaths in the U.S. by the end of May, people started inching out, even with social distancing rules still in place. But the States and Cities took dramatically different approaches as to how quickly or slowly they reopened. The result was a confusing quilt of mask requirements and regulations, usually dependent on whether the governing authority was Democratic or Republican. The federal government by this time had abandoned any unified consistent response outside of throwing money at the crisis.

But bit by bit, the country reopened in spite of itself. It was a rocky reopening, like a car engine, trying to turn over. But eventually, it did.

Yet for every 2 steps forward, there were at least 1 and 1/2 steps back. The upcoming 2020 presidential election was even more brutal than even the crazy 2016 election. An angry President Trump who could see his election prospects slipping away, refused to promise that he would accept the results of the election. The country was split and seethed.

Then, on May 25, 2020, George Floyd died in Minneapolis. All over a counterfeit $20 bill presented at a small store.

His death tore the scab of racial injustice wide open. By May 26, despite the still required current social distancing in many states, millions of Americans protested peacefully against the horrible manner in which his death occurred. But in several cities, the protests turned into riots and in Minneapolis alone there was over $200,000,000 dollars' worth of damage. Lake Street there, looked like a war zone. Instead of bringing the country together, President Trump forcefully cleared Lafayette Park of peaceful protesters with tear gas in Washington D.C. Steve started referring to the President as: "Our Divider in Chief." Such was the stressed, politically, overheated summer of 2020.

The Fall of 2020 with the Federal Presidential Election failed to lower the nation's temperature. Quite the opposite. The political fever would not break. The country remained divided and split. President Trump continued to decline to commit to a peaceful transfer of power after the election. He continued to make baseless accusations on the integrity of the Nation's election system, which was conducted by the States. After all, he was behind in the polls and how could that be? On November 3rd, 2020, President Trump lost the election to Joe Biden in both the popular vote and the Electoral College. President Trump refused to accept the results and entertained crazy theories on how to remain in power.

Still, there was some good news later in the Fall. The first Covid Vaccine made by Pfizer was approved by The FDA on December 11, 2020. (Again, see Timeline.) Steve and others felt, maybe, just maybe, they had finally turned the corner and life was looking up.

But like the rest of the year, the calm was short lived. The Nation's political fever started rising again. On December 19, the President encouraged his millions of followers to come to Washington to protest the election results: "Be there. Be Wild!" Tens of thousands came on January 6,2021. The day he invited them was the same day, Congress was set to officially certify Joe Biden's victory in the Electoral College.

The thousands of protesters turned into a mob and the capitol was over run. Out of control, the riot led to the deaths of 5 people. Over 140 Police Officers were injured protecting the elected representatives. After hours of hand-to-hand combat, the House and Senate finally reconvened in the dead of night, did their duty, and Joe Biden was certified as the next U.S. President.

On January 20, 2021, Joe Biden was inaugurated as the next president and the long political nightmare began to ease. But not enough. By February 1, 2021, more Americans were vaccinated than not. For those who were vaccinated, life after covid was becoming a reality. Sadly, given the country's divisions, it was not surprising that a significant part of the population, roughly 1/3, believed it was their right to refuse to get a vaccine. Studies showed that a person was 10 times more likely to die of Covid if they were not vaccinated. But no matter. It was still THEIR body and their choice. By May 17, U.S. Covid deaths exceeded 1,000,000 people. It was beyond sad. Heartbreaking. Millions carried the heavy silent pain of loved lost ones, gone too soon and too quickly. But for the majority, they were already looking forward to life A.C. i.e., after Covid.

With the return to the new normal, people started going out again, meeting again, making plans again.

Joe, surprisingly at age 72, wanted to repurchase his old business and viewed the return from Covid as a business opportunity. But then again, he liked to look at himself as an opportunistic optimist. Or maybe it was the other way around. He certainly had the energy for it. Joe looked like he was in his mid-60's.

Stu was starting yet another low carb diet. He was a thoughtful guy who was far too serious when he got into something. Stu knew he had delayed too many somethings because of Covid. Excuse time was over.

Ted had planned a trip back to Ireland with Grace to see friends that he hadn't seen in 3 years. Zoom didn't count.

Tim was going to turn over the real estate to the kids. Finally. It was time to see if they could swim or sink.

Ralph was planning on entering an International Tango Competition with Jackie on Zoom. He had picked up a free mannequin at a closed Marshall Field's Department Store's Dumpster after the Coffee Guys convinced him that it would look odd to do an intimate dance with a fake Roomba. (Sorry, Jackie) Tim had figured out how to mount the female mannequin temporarily on Jackie (which Ralph now claimed was short for Jacqueline) so she could practice Tango and still get her cleaning work done. Ralph had even gone out and commissioned matching Spanish Outfits. Ralph promised to share the Zoom link when it became available. Ralph was confident they would "clean up" at the competition. While bizarre, Ralph had not been this happy in years.

Fred was going to finish cleaning his work garage- no easy feat. It was over 1,000 square feet, crammed with every tool and work machine imaginable. If a loyal subscriber to Popular Mechanics died and went to Heaven, Fred's garage is where they would want to spend eternity. No kidding. His wife Beth was a Saint. For sure.

Russ was finally ready to move forward on that Greek restaurant he had thought about opening for years. Like a lot of people who thought about their plans, Russ felt Covid delayed would turn into Covid denied if he wasn't careful.

And Theo was gonna fly on that silver airplane tube to visit his older sister in Florida. Time hadn't been waiting.

The boys refined their plans almost every day at coffee, reminding themselves later at home that free advice was sometimes only worth what a person paid for it. In other words, nothing.

Unlike the other guys, Steve knew he was not in a position yet to make plans. He was well aware of that old saying: "Wanna make God laugh? Make Plans." Steve wondered when he could bring up his cancer diagnosis. Other guys in the group had been forthright in discussing their run ins with cancer, but Steve was used to keeping things pretty close to his vest. It was a lot easier but heavier that way. He knew his wife Ann was right, usually was, that you got to talk about things. But a lot of guys didn't typically do that. But smart guys do.

Steve decided to give it a go when it was just the two of them:

"So, Theo, remember that Doctor's visit I had a couple weeks ago, well the results are back and they ain't good. I've got Prostate Cancer. Again."

Theo blinked twice, reflected for a bit, then: "How bad? Is it worse than the Prostate Cancer you had before?"

Steve swallowed. Prostate Cancer ran in his family. His Dad and Uncle Moses had in fact died from Prostate Cancer. Steve had been watching his PSA count for years: "Well…. Apparently, my good looks are not the only thing I inherited from my Dad. It's not good."

Theo put his arm around Steve's shoulder. He was old enough that he wasn't afraid to hug someone: "Cancer ain't as bad as it used to be. Hey Lou had Prostate Cancer and he's doing ok."

"I got it bad. The industrial strength kind this time. Stage 4."

"Hey, you'll beat this thing. You gonna swallow some of those radioactive pumpkin seeds?"

Sometimes Theo did get his facts out of order. Radioactive pellets, called "seeds", that were used to treat the Prostrate were typically inserted on the other end through the urethra.

Steve smiled at Theo's mistake. For some reason, it cheered him back up: "Theo, you're right and its only Tuesday. (Steve liked to joke that at times it took Theo til Thursday to get a fact right.) I gotta beat this thing so you guys got some adult supervision."

"You start taking that vinegar daily like I said?" Theo had a strange mystical belief in the restorative powers of vinegar.

"I'm working on it." Steve did not share Theo's confidence in the foul-tasting drink. Or for that matter, Theo's Omega 3 vitamin suggestion that you protect your brain by the daily consumption of the smallest, stinkiest sardines you could swallow. If Theo

33

wasn't a self-taught home remedy doctor, he was at least, a pharmacist. Where did he come up with these ideas? Maybe he took his cues from President Trump who suggested trying bleach to cure Covid. Seriously?

"You take care of yourself, we ain't done educating you yet." Theo had always felt that Steve's college degrees had only gotten in the way of his true education about life. Steve thought Theo might be right. Sometimes the piles of books he read blocked his view of available common-sense solutions. Only sometimes. They pushed in the chairs and walked away.

3. We All Had Losses, Some Remain Lost.

Steve jumped into his car, a black Toyota Hybrid Highlander and drove off. It wasn't an attractive car like his old 2012 Cadillac SRX with its expansive moonroof, but at least it wasn't a mini-van. Like the other members of his coffee club, Steve had taken an unspoken vow to never drive another minivan now that their kids were grown up. Steve was lucky that Ann was so tolerant of Steve's incurable and constant automotive lust.

Though he had things to do, he decided to take the long way back and took Sheridan Road north towards Willamette. The Lake and then Northwestern University campus came into view with its jarring mixture of sedate, ivy-covered buildings and stark modern structures, then the magnificent Bahai Temple. The Temple, one of only seven in the world, was a tall white curved structure that looked like a wide, standing on end, cloud or as Ann liked to say, the world's largest soft serve ice cream cone. Steve parked his car and walked the grounds. Though Steve didn't know much about the Bahai faith other than it was founded in Persia in the 1800's, he found the Temple grounds and especially the structure very peaceful.

Steve watched a bunny stop and freeze in place before scampering off. It reminded Steve of how all coffee club members tried to needle their way through Covid. Like everyone else, they all heard the rumors about the vague threat in the early days of January 2020. At first, they ignored it, then froze, not knowing where to go. Then, as the threat and deaths grew closer, by March under the mandatory quarantines, they stayed in their rabbit holes. Ultimately, they withdrew into themselves and their close immediate family. It was a scary and threatening time. The inconsistent and bizarre approaches of state and federal leaders only made it worse.

Steve found a metal bench and sat down. In spite of the 10,000 steps he took a day, he was sitting more often. Pausing. Reflecting. Forgetting. Maybe he was losing it a bit. He could no longer simply remember everything he needed to- like his calendar. He would misplace it everywhere and this was the paper device that was supposed to keep him on track. Ann would laugh and tell him that it was "Sometimers, not Alzheimer's", his occasional forgetfulness was a natural part of aging." Well, Steve was determined to resist the aging process as much as he could and took to writing things down. Problem was he could not write EVERYTHING down even if he was a late blooming writer. Besides, he would find his written notes EVERYWHERE with no sense or logic to them. Worse yet, sometimes, even he couldn't read his own handwriting. Ann was kind enough to act as his personal member of the National Archives, sorting through his maze of papers, asking which ones needed to be maintained and which ones could be recycled.

Steve glanced at his watch. Still liked to wear one even if he didn't need it most of the time. His kids had all given up wearing watches. They kept track of their time and everything else going on in the world with their phones. Steve was different. He carried his phone but wasn't tethered to it. Most of the time, which as a semi-retired soul, he had plenty of- he kept the ringer off. If it was an important call, they would leave a message. His older friend Marv tried the opposite approach- If he was available, he would answer his phone. If he wasn't or it was inconvenient, he wouldn't. No voicemail for him. Why bother? Either he was available, or he wasn't.

Steve had time. Lately, he had been ruminating, a lot, over the Covid "stuff". Steve spent a lot of time thinking about how he and Ann had made it through Covid and why others had not. It wasn't fair. Some glided through, in spite of taking few precautions, and others died a painful death. Sometimes, it had something to do with pre-existing conditions like weight, diabetes or asthma. For some reason, the elderly suffered more serious outcomes. In the end, it was luck (mazel). Who had it and who didn't. While they really didn't talk about it much at coffee, Theo warned him more than once that he was wasting too much of his life, wondering about the why's and not the how's. While this sounded good, Steve didn't understand what Theo meant. He wasn't sure Theo did either. That was Ok. In any case, everyone had to find their own way. Some never did.

For Steve, he realized he had been lucky. He and Ann hadn't lost any close relatives or friends and spent most of the Covid quarantine in 2020 in Sedona, Arizona. They had been careful, i.e., masking, social distancing, no indoor restaurants, no going to friends' homes but still… Sedona was not a bad place to be marooned while the world tried in fits and starts to sort out the existential crisis of Covid. Most days this was not an issue for Steve as he spent most of his time hiking the trails while Ann took advantage of the many Temple classes and book clubs over Zoom. Ann had never met a Temple she hadn't enjoyed so she was a member of three of them. As Ann was wont to say: "How could you get too much of a good thing? " Well, Steve could and often did. He joked that he suffered from Spiritual Bloating. Steve was content to search for his spirituality such as it was, hiking at the Cathedral Rock Trail.

Before Steve knew it was 10:43 am and he still needed to clean up his act or more specifically his park so off he went.

4. Indian Boundary Park.

Steve drove back and was lucky enough to find street parking on Fitch Avenue. Parking was a major hassle in the Windy City. Most of the homes and apartments in the city were built before World War Two in a time when many Chicago residents still relied on public transportation instead of private cars. As a result, apartments were not required to have any off-street parking. But times had changed, and many car owners suffered from a well-deserved case of parking envy. Even after owning his apartment unit for over 6 years, Steve and Ann still had not graduated to the limited parking on site. It was a sore spot for both of them, especially Steve. Ann believed Steve had an advanced case of Parking Lust.

But the park, Indian Boundary Park which adjoined their home was a joy. Named after the Peace Treaty, it was a small park. Just 13 acres, it had been built on what had been the western boundary of the city. The Peace Treaty was signed in 1816 between the Odawa, Ojibwe and Potawatomi Tribes and the U.S. as to what lands would be open to U.S. settlement. It was yet another treaty with the Natives that was had not been

honored by the United States. The actual, original boundary
line was in the park. Approximately 100 years later, the present
park was built in the 1920s. It had a petting zoo (long gone),
a pond that ducks and turtles frequented, a bear water spray
feature, fallen climbing trees and its chief claim to fame, a volunteer built climbing structure that had many a hiding spot where
young children could secretly observe their adoring parents. It
was one of a few remaining wooden climbing structures in the
Chicago Park District. Unfortunately, after 30 years of heavy
use, the playground had far outlived its useful life. Wood was
rotting, posts were sagging and there were so many wooden
slivers, that Steve had taken to carrying band aids in his wallet
for emergencies. The decaying structure was a sad metaphor
for the condition of the park. The problem was that during the
Pandemic, the park got even more use and less clean. Frankly,
it began looking like a dirty third world garbage pit with garbage,
dirty diapers, beer cans and the like all over the park. It frustrated Steve that the park was one of the few outdoor areas readily
accessible to the public during the Pandemic, and was treated
or more accurately, abused this way. Eventually, Steve began
to follow his son in law's example and ordered his own personal

garbage picker and started picking up garbage in the park. It was amazing how therapeutic it felt to leave a cleaner park for everyone who frequented it.

It had been frustrating to see the inexorable decline of the park. The park had literally been left to rot. Collapsed trees, thinning grass that had been overtaken by weeds. Broken pipes left rusting on the grounds for years. (Steve knew this because he had, unsuccessfully, tried to move the pipe on his own.) It seemed to be an allegory for the city. What isn't maintained, goes to Hell. Sometimes it drags the city dwellers down there with them.

Yet still, there was some lingering spark that continued to draw people of all ages to the park. People had a longing for nature. Some days, it would draw over 500 people. The Park had a calming effect on most people. Steve felt it was Nature's prescription for better health. Perhaps. Or maybe, it was the memories of playing on the same playground equipment that their parents did? Could have even been, sitting on the same old wooden bench that their grandparents did. The same sidewalks still existed that led one from the ponds to the former site of the small zoo to the tennis courts still in use.

There was a familiar comfort when people of every age hung out at the park- kind of like a comfort zone or a reassuring hug from an elderly grandparent. No way was Steve gonna let this park slide on this day into further decay. He felt good doing his part, keeping the trash under a semblance of control. So, after only 43 minutes of picking up trash and trying to convince some other grandparents to do the same, at the playground, his work was done, and he walked across the park to his home.

5. The Mostly Cooperative Life.

Steve and Ann had found their Chicago home by accident. When their daughter Rita was pregnant, Ann informed Steve that she had a physical need to live by her grandchildren. Living in Minneapolis at the time, Steve laughed and thought Ann was kidding. She was not. It was as if self-regulating genetic grandma switch had gone on in his wife. The closer their daughter Rita came to delivering, the more frequent these discussions of the necessity of living by the grandchildren during their formative years became. Almost like a mantra. Being a simple prospective grandpa, Steve thought he could love his grandchildren from afar, kinda like some grandfather version of ESP. Nope. So, ten years ago, they started looking for an appropriate Bubbe's (grandma) nest within easy walking distance of their daughter's home. After all, they wanted to live close but not too close. Steve no longer wanted to live in a house, especially if they were gone during winter. Chicago had a well-deserved reputation of being a personal injury attorney heaven with all the slips and falls during the typical, icy winter. Some of the lawyers had prearranged, automatic TV ads for when the temperature fell between 30- and 42-degrees Fahrenheit. Anyways, the search for a home was long and arduous. They despaired, well at least Steve despaired enough for the two of them, of ever finding an appropriate condo or apartment in the West Rogers Park neighborhood. Much of the housing was tired, more like exhausted, and not kept up. Ann planning for their future fragility, guilty of smart thinking, wanted an elevator building so they wouldn't have to take the stairs. This meant a serious look at the 14 story Winston Towers, which to Steve looked like they had been designed by a Communist East German Architect with a migraine. Steve took to walking all streets in the neighborhood, desperately searching for an appropriate abode that wasn't so damn depressing. Another requirement was it had to be within walking distance of their future generations, i.e. grandkids. Then, one Friday afternoon, about 4 pm, he came across the Ladies of the Vine, having their regular happy hour in the gazebo at the Park Gables. The ladies had been given their honorific title for the frequent happy hours they held in the cozy alcove. Aptly named, the ladies, Sima (Hebrew for treasure) and Rose (For Rose) were women of a mature age and youthful spirit. They were welcoming to everyone they met, and Sima even had a daily hug for the malodorous (fancy way of saying stinky.) garbage-man Max. Sima said people didn't stink- only their politics did. After Steve called them over that fateful afternoon, it was Sima that let them into the building and let them know about the soon to be available first floor unit. Steve and Ann were eternally grateful to Sima for her help.

The Park Gables was a large Tudor Revival Complex that took up one full city block with only 72 residences. Built in 1927, it was one of the first cooperatives in Chicago, located adjacent to Indian Boundary Park. Steve and Ann understood coops. In fact, they then lived in a Coop in Minneapolis. Coops were usually older owner-occupied buildings that predated the Uniform Condominium Act. Owners owned Coop stock shares that gave them the right to inhabit specific apartments. Financing for coops was more difficult with a larger down payment required and prospective shareholders had to be interviewed/approved by other shareholders. It was for most purposes, a quirky condominium adventure, and coop residents often stayed there for decades. It was a magnificent structure that had been meticulously maintained by the current shareholders for the benefit of future owners. Coop members were good that way.

Shareholders looked out for each other and their building. In fact, many shareholders convinced their relatives or friends to move in. It was that special of a place. But what was quirky to some- could be annoying to others. Like any aging, fragile parent, the Park Gables needed a lot of continuing (read expensive) maintenance. Steve and Ann dreaded the day the indoor Roman Pool also built in 1927, had to be replaced. After all, it was complete with white Terracotta Doric columns and antique tile floors. And the noise? The Gables were built in a time before sound engineering was a thing. What this meant was shareholders might hear their neighbors in everything from private conversations to flushing the toilet. Living at the building was a continuing, intimate, sound experience with the neighbors. Everyone, really did know everything about their neighbors. EVERYTHING.

Coop members had gotten through the Pandemic pretty well, all things considered. Members really did look out for each other. Shareholders would share books, food, takeout dinners from restaurants, and the remarkable bounty from their individual garden plots. Others would give rides to medical appointments and other necessary things. Perhaps most importantly, coop members kept an eye on the physical and emotional health of their neighbors. People were always willing to lend a shoulder to lean on and when necessary to cry on during the Pandemic. Members would sit outside at the Gazebo or on the picnic benches, sometimes talking into the night. Others would go for long or short walks usually at the park. The park was right next door, literally, as there was no street between the park and the Gables and the nature was balm to the aching souls. Some shareholders would leave their windows open to hear the children, romping at the playground. Others would take a favorite book and read at a park bench. Many soothed their souls with dirt, digging, sorting, pruning, reminding themselves, that their gardens would still grow. While there were sad losses, significant losses of loved ones- their community held. They and their community at the Gables had survived.

6. Ann and Steve.

Looking back, Steve found being back at the coop to be more restrictive and onerous on their freedom than being in Arizona. It wasn't the Coop's fault; it was a fact of living back in the big city. Steve and Ann were cognizant of how fortunate they were compared to many others. Yes, they now had their grandkids and conveniences nearby, but Steve missed the open spaces and the true quiet of the Sedona hiking trails. Ann quickly slotted back into her previous role of family guidance counselor, like she had just returned from a long-term leave of absence-even when at first, she couldn't hug them. Steve? Not so much. He was glad to be back and loved the kids, but he still missed daily interaction with the Red Rocks of Sedona. It was a relief when the country started to open up again and he, at least, had the coffee club to go back to.

Then there was the whole question of how much "together" time Ann and Steve needed or even wanted. While Ann was content to withdraw within and quietly read a book alone, for Steve, a people person by nature, it was constant tension as to how much time- was too much or too little time together. Too much?

Too little? He wanted to be supportive- but not too supportive. It really was a constant balancing act. He was almost relieved when Ann sent him outside to play or in his case- hike. They were good that way to each other.

Others had a much tougher go as a couple during Covid. Family losses, job losses, health and financial concerns, all added heavy stress to relationships. But somehow, Steve and Ann stumbled through, most of the time, happily. Then, there were the ones who had to carry heavier burdens than anyone should bear. They had lost beloved parents, spouses, children and friends. Still, they had to carry on. Or at least try to…

The guys at coffee regularly talked about how they had handled the quarantine/ pandemic: after the coffee sessions at Cera's resumed. They all had different approaches:

Fred kept busy, real busy, sorting out his springs and screws in his garage. He had already finished sharpening up his tools. He dreamed of the day; he could resume the search for his Corvette engine that was sitting at the bottom of the Mississippi

River. Fred had plans to install it in his unrestored 1983 Olds-mobile Vista Cruiser. For now, he had to make do, with tooling around in his dark blue, slightly dented Chevrolet Tahoe.

Stu, though he still traded in stocks occasionally, what he really traded daily, in now, was binge watching TV. For his waistline's credit, he had installed a home gym for daily exercise that kept him physically and emotionally healthy.

Ted had a lifetime of memories to sort through and it was power of Grace, his loving partner, that literally, made it happen. He finally let go of his treasured Chicago Daily news collection including its Mayor Daley funeral coverage.

Parking Paul still had his squirrels, every day he was out there at Warren Park. He liked to joke that he was nuts about their antics. In Paul's opinion, it was far superior than the cute kitten videos on YouTube.

Joe, like he joked, his recently repurchased business was plug-ging along. He liked to brag that he was plunging to new depths of success.

Russ had difficult choices as a father and husband. As a store manager, he had even more issues. Masking, enough staffing, angry customers, thefts, shortages- it was several migraines every day.

Tim still had, what he called his second wife, his real estate business. Unlike his classy wife Sal, the real estate always nagged and pulled on him. Like most of the guys, including Steve, Tim had married up.

Then, there what Theo called the "Floaters", those who floated in and floated out, irregularly. Some continued to show up on occasion. Others were never seen again without explanation. Guys were like that. People could and did fall off the face of the earth. That was not a healthy thing to do.

Thankfully their kids never did. Jan and Ray, Rita and Saul, Phil and Lori all showed a remarkable ability to show up every day, and just do what they had to do to get their families through these extraordinary times. Literally, they had to dance on the head of a pin every day and never fall off. They were flexible and determined. Each day, they did what needed to be done. No more and no less. They all threaded an invisible thread with grace and fortitude. Their kids made it through with their emotional and physical health intact. No one could ask for anything more. But yet- Covid did. Every day. And so, Jan and Ray, Rita and Saul, Phil and Lori responded as the times required.

7. Anne and Steve Make a Run for it.

There had been no great, well thought out plan as to when to go back to Chicago. Steve woke up one day, Summer of 2021, and knew they needed to get back. Right away! The ache in his soul told him so. It started at 4 am. That it was Steve who wanted to leave NOW was somewhat surprising, for it was Ann who talked the most about missing the kids, meaning the grandkids, often. They had tried zooming and telephone calls, but it wasn't the same. Not even close.

As with everything else in Arizona, that was Covid related in the Winter of 2021, the distribution of vaccines was haphazard and inconsistent. It was a similar problem in other states. When the vaccines first came out, their friends in Minnesota participated in a gold rush, desperately seeking, the lifesaving vaccines. Friends were traveling hundreds of miles from Minneapolis to Fargo or Duluth to get the magic shot. Everyone would rush to wherever they heard there was a supply and people were certainly not above using a connection to get it. The general population was desperate enough and would do and often- did do anything to jump ahead of the line. People wanted to live and by now, people were aware that individuals in their 60's were more susceptible, read more likely, to be killed by the virus.

In Arizona, Steve and Ann found it impossible to get a shot in Phoenix, which was the closest large metropolitan area to Sedona. Every time they attempted to register for the shot, the computerized reservations systems would overload into a never-ending circle of death on the laptop screen. Trying to register at what he thought would be a less crowded time at 3 am, a tired Steve thought the death circles were appropriate. Ironically, what got Steve and Ann the vaccine was a combination of their neighbors and anti-vaxxers. One day in late January 2021, Steve received a call from Sue who lived next door. She explained that she and her husband had gotten the shots at a church in Cottonwood and that they had open appointments. Steve later surmised that demand for the shots was not as great in the higher Republican rural areas that had a higher percentage of anti-vaxxers. After telling Sue, she was a real-life saver, Steve quickly made appointments for himself and Ann. After getting the shots, Steve felt the vaccination card was a passport to future days.

By February 1, 2021, more people were vaccinated nationwide than were not. Still large numbers of people died needlessly for exercising their "right" not to get vaccinated. Many of these people refused to wear masks or socially distance themselves. This Freedom to Refuse played a significant role with the population not reaching a herd immunity. So, the deaths kept on coming. By February 22, 2021, U.S. Covid deaths exceeded 300,000. By May 17, 2021, the death toll exceeded 1,000,000. It was and remains in some ways incomprehensible. Preventable. Tragic.

But for people who took the shots and practiced reasonable caution (i.e., social distancing, masks in indoor places, eating outside), life was getting to be more reminiscent of the days before the Pandemic.

So, Steve and Ann had started thinking about when they could return to Chicago. After all, they hadn't seen their kids in almost 2 years. They watched the Covid maps detailing daily positivity rates like daily weather reports. In spite of the immense death toll, it still felt like the Covid Fever had broken in the Spring of 2021.

So, one day that summer, Steve woke up and knew his whole body was telling him- it was time to go. Time to make a run for it. It was an almost a physical need. An ache, a hunger. He now better understood how Ann, the Zooming Bubbe felt. Experiencing the grandchildren's growth was an unbreakable string or connection. Ann had, of course, been ready to go since they left for Sedona, two years ago. So now, in a quick frenzy, they packed up and left that afternoon. Their car took Hwy 179 and left the Red Rocks in their rear-view mirror. Before they knew it, they were at US I-17. They went North towards Flagstaff. While it seemed strange to drive North before driving East, the beautiful Pines were welcoming. Less than an hour later, they had already turned East onto I-40 and the typography changed again, more flat and dusty. After about 200 miles, Ann had long been ready to quit for the night. But Steve was a driver on a mission. Finally, they made it to Albuquerque, New Mexico where Steve reluctantly stopped for the night. Only 330 miles for the first day.

The grandparent adrenaline surge had evaporated somewhere before Winslow, Arizona. They were really going have to up the daily pace if they were gonna make it home. They still had 1300 miles to go.

The next 2 long days were a black and white blur of crummy take-out food and dirty gas station bathrooms as they traveled the hundreds of necessary miles. Steve called it sleep driving, which was a little scary, but accurate description of how he felt. Not really awake, not really there. Just moving as quickly as they could. Wanting, needing to get back. Throughout the trip, gas stations and Mc Donald's Drive thru lines were busy. Real Busy. More people were finally moving about the country. Must have been all the grandparent snowbirds finally migrating back up North. But they were coming ever closer to Chicago. After two long days, they were closing in. That final third day, they were "only" 600 miles away. They stared at their map. Still had the Ozarks, Springfield (Missouri), Rolla, St. Louis, Springfield (Illinois), Bloomington, Pontiac, Joliet to go before being swallowed up by Chicago. They could do this. They kept driving, they kept pushing. Finally, they staggered into their apartment in the dark of night. Must have been 2 or 3 am. For a brief moment, Steve feared they were in the wrong unit. Thankfully, not.

They were home and Ann was convinced that her grandchildren were already aware. Again, that vaunted Bubbe (Grandma) ESP at work yet again. More important, Steve and Ann both knew it was right to be back. That affirmation was all their bodies needed to know. Body systems began their shutdown mode immediately. They fell asleep quickly.

8. Back Where They Sort of Belong.

The next day, Ann woke up early and celebrated by making a large feta cheese omelet. She was happy to be in her familiar surroundings after being on the road for almost 2000 miles. She was even willing to add canned mushrooms that Steve enjoyed in his eggs. Like many items in their pantry, the canned mushrooms were probably expired as a result of the two of them having been gone so long. But Ann figured the expiration date was only a suggestion and not a legal mandate. During Covid, consumers had gotten back to just making do with things they had. Ann was grateful that she had brought her remaining treasured feta cheese that she ate on her salads and her omelets every day. Steve had his preferences too, and maybe now that they were back in town, he could return to his favorite spicy cheese from Costco. While being marooned in Sedona during Covid, they both spent a fair amount of time discussing what products they missed most due to production shortages and those dang hoarders. In Sedona with the limited shopping options, toilet paper and paper towels had to be rationed by the one grocery store in town. Ann was happy as long as she had access to some sort of feta cheese while for Steve, hot sauce and instant coffee was all he needed. After all, Costco was almost 60 miles away in Prescott. Fortunately, they had generous neighbors who also liked to trade. Back in Chicago, scarcity should have been less of an issue, though by 6:30 am, Ann had already texted her daughters to see if they wanted anything from Costco and as all-knowing Bubbe, texted several suggestions. That they need-ed things from Costco, Ann was sure of, but whether they would allow their mother to select it or make what Ann considered acceptable substitutions was another matter entirely. Steve had long ago given up on trying to referee the Costco tug of war be-tween Ann and their daughters but had the good fortune to buy Costco stock many years ago after being frustrated at the cost of a particularly large and costly Costco run. Steve figured if you couldn't beat them, you could at least buy them. (The stock, that is.) So, he did.

Steve on the other hand, made other plans. He was looking for-ward to seeing at least some of the guys somehow or, at least, getting outdoors. So, he took his Ebike over to Dunkin Donuts because he wanted to stretch his legs (no pedal assist today) and the bike gave him an excuse not to carry coffee. He took the 4 sugared donuts, (why buy extra?) and took a safe route on Bell Street to Theo's back yard on Morse Avenue. Steve had managed to arrange delivery of the Ebike in Sedona. With the awesome views due to the frequent hills, the Ebike was a real leg saver in the hilly Red Rocks. He hoped to bike a lot in Chicago. Bike parking was easier than trying to find a place to stash a car. Usually, but not always.

Theo lived in a nice brick two story town home that was commonplace in the 1980's. Brick was big in Chicago ever since the Great Chicago Fire of 1871. That tradition of building with brick carried on to the present day. Steve punched in the still current security code to the garage (Heck, he and Theo were still that close), and pulled out four plastic lawn chairs. Only then, since it was after 7 am, did he softly knock on the door. Theo's wife Fran was probably still asleep. Steve had no doubt that Theo was already up. After all he had run a convenience store for decades and often had to take over a no-show employee shift. Theo was such a poor sleeper that he kept a police scanner to keep abreast of the neighborhood troubles on those frequent nights he couldn't sleep. After all, he was still the unelected mayor of Western Avenue. Steve was right:

"Hey, you're back. How was the drive?"

"Thorough." So was Steve's answer: "I brought donuts. Dunkin. Can you make coffee?"

"What's a matter, too cheap to spring for coffee, too?" (Fair point, Dunkin Donuts did have good coffee.)

"I rode my bike and didn't wanna spill it. Besides, I am not cheap, I'm just value oriented."

"Cheap, cheap, cheap."

Steve didn't like the sound of that: "I will stipulate to being frugal." After all both Ann and he had grown up poor or as Steve liked to put it- fiscally challenged.

"All right, call it what you will. I got some Maxwell House coffee here somewhere to brew."

"I pulled out 4 chairs, that gonna be enough?" From the emails he had received, Steve knew that morning coffee attendance had dwindled since they had been meeting outside, regardless of whether they met at Cera's grocery store or Theo's backyard. People were still well worn out from battling Covid and some were still not comfortable meeting inside at first, vaccinated or not.

Rick stumbled in carrying his obligatory, personal donut and coffee from 7-11. Steve who hadn't seen him in several years showed him no mercy: "Good to see your 7-11 diet is still working for you." This is how guys showed they cared- by shoveling healthy amounts of abuse at each other. What an unhealthy amount of verbal abuse was unclear.

Rick had probably worked the late shift at Excusi Me Pizza, delivering late night needed carbo loads (pizza): "Good to see you, too." Rick was perpetually tired.

Most guys in general including this group, had a hard time expressing their feelings. But at least this group had some. The three sat around Theo's outdoor dining set. It was like Steve had never left:

"You ever finish that mystery novel about the bank robbery?" Rick directed his question to Steve who had been working on a novel during Covid like the 730,000 other budding novelists. Apparently some 300,000 novels had been self-published during the Pandemic. Steve had been working semi-diligently on a book about a group of public utility workers who decided to break into the basement safety deposit box room of a major midwestern bank when the workers were replacing the sewer line. Their friend Ted was serving as an unofficial advisor to Steve regarding all underground issues. But the more Steve dug into the project, the more stuck he seemed to get. While Steve had promised himself that he wouldn't return to Chicago until he finished a complete first draft, he felt jammed up and was hopeful, by returning to the scene of the crime, he might be inspired to make some real progress. Or at least, inspired. Lately, in Sedona he had been avoiding working on his novel at all. It was simply one of those things, it was easier to talk about versus actually do. Steve had read that 97% of all people who start writing a novel never finish it. He was determined to be part of that lucky 3%, that completed their goal, no matter what it took.

Just then Ted walked in, again reminding Steve of what he needed to do: "Got my book done yet?" Ted being a pipefitter, was enthralled with the project. He was hopeful it would give working stiffs, people that worked with their hands, their proper due: "Thought you might be here. I got something here for your book. Been carrying it around, waiting for you to show up." Ted pulled something from his pocket, it was a small, faded Saint figure. Steve had been around long enough to know what it was from previous real estate transactions: "Your St. Joseph statute won't work on me, I'm Jewish, remember?" St. Joseph was believed by devout Catholics to assist in the sale of homes. Apparently, Ted believed it could assist in the sale of a novel.

"You never know." Ted said defensively: "St. Joseph protects even you from harm, you know." When Ted got defensive, his

Irish brogue accent got stronger. "Just bury it in your building's front yard and it will help sell your book to a publisher." Ted knew how hard Steve had tried to get a real literary agent before resorting to self-actualization (i.e. self-publication) for his last three books. Ted was a believer in Steve but not naïve enough to believe one could make a best seller on their own.

"It won't work on me, I'm Jewish and I can't bury it in the front yard without the permission of the 71 other shareholders who own Park Gables units with me. Besides I already got a Mezuzah up on my front door to protect us. "

"Think of it as insurance. Don't forget to plant it upside down as per Irish custom. Think of it as an additional umbrella policy." Ted, a smart guy, knew his insurance.

"The Mezuzah has our holiest prayer, so I think we're good." Steve didn't need to add that, but he had a competitive soul and figured God who is mentioned in the prayer outranked a Saint. But you never know. Maybe, just maybe, it might help.

"You know belt AND suspenders never hurt." Ted had a point. Well, sometimes, they do but not here. Steve finally recognized the kind gesture for what it was:

"I'll get up early and plant him in the dirt, first thing in the morning." Everyone was happy, even Steve who had grown up in the city of Saint Paul, Minnesota. Who was he to ignore possible heaven-based assistance?

The donuts went quickly. Steve wasn't gonna have one but with the newly brewed coffee, it was almost a no brainer. Or he could have said: "A stomach gainer." After all what the stomach wants, the stomach usually gets- diet or no diet.

Steve was curious how the two guys had gotten through the long dark night called Covid, especially the single guys like Rick. The zooming and texting hadn't been the same as the regular face to face conversations.

Surprisingly, Rick had done pretty well. Not that Steve didn't have confidence in Rick's ability to get by, but face it, a married couple had a built-in support network. Or so, it should be. Perhaps, that explained why the rate of divorce fell during the height of Covid. People were hunkering down with what they had. Hopefully, for the better.

Rick explained that he had kept quite busy with work and school during the quarantine and thereafter. People still had to eat and he still needed to learn. So, he polished off the BA in history quickly, virtually all on zoom. Now he was working towards a Master's. For emotional support, he still had family nearby including a brother who was useful for hijinks.

Ted had his wife Grace, and they were splendid together, even during adverse occasions. They had managed to stay close to all of their three children, two of which were police officers and one who had become an attorney. Ted liked to joke that there was a black sheep in every family.

Then there was Theo. Theo had managed well during the crisis. Driving his trusty Kia steed, he still made his daily rounds. Of course, he and his wife Gwen were still able to get out and about. No pandemic was going to slow Theo down. As a long time, proud self-employed business owner, Theo thought it was his patriotic duty to continue to support the local, family-owned restaurants. It was clear that they needed the help and then some. Even though people were no longer barred from eating inside restaurants, many people preferred to still eat outside or get takeout. So, most nights, Theo and Gwen would jump in their car and go for a drive until they found an open restaurant. Sometimes, they had to stop at 2 or 3 closed restaurants before they found a surviving diner. As all restaurant owners knew, life wasn't fair, especially during Covid.

That was then. Now, restaurants were packed…Customers had a lot of deferred gluttony to catch up with. The remaining open restaurants eagerly complied with the digestive needs of their clients.

To celebrate the new openness, the gang decided to set up a breakfast several months later at the Batter Up Pancake House up in Evanston. As usual, Joe made the reservation with Ava the hostess. Ava was part of the attraction of the restaurant for she made everyone feel welcome and was even willing to give up several tables during prime breakfast hours for long-time patrons. Steve was glad her restaurant had made it. Besides the good food and service, the fact that Ava's family owned the building, in addition to the restaurant, gave them extra breathing space during the dark days.

Looked like a pretty good turnout that Steve observed when he purposedly showed up late on his Ebike. Through the plate glass window, he saw that even Beatrice had made an appearance. He tried to remember just how long it had been since he had seen some of these rascals. His memory wasn't as sharp, or at least was more dull after meandering through Covid times. After thanking Ava for putting up with the group, Steve made his way through the crowded restaurant to the rear two tables. Everyone was eagerly talking, not listening and contrary to what they had promised their wives, no one was wearing a mask. Nor were most of the other patrons, though Ava was smart enough to require the wait staff be masked. While customers might be replaced, the more valuable, experienced restaurant staff could not, especially now.

"Well Mr. Ebike, nice of you to show up. What's the matter, your battery wear out? Have to walk to get here?" Ava had always been quick with a quip.

"Nope, I've got plenty of juice. More than I can say about those pacemaker batteries you pick up at the dollar store." The best defense was a good and unyielding offense. Especially with this group. Steve grabbed a chair next to Beatrice. He remembered Bea was short for Beatrice but he wasn't sure:

"Beatrice, good to see you, how long has it been?" It had been so long since most people had seen each other, that they couldn't remember just how long it had been. People forgot what friends looked like. It just was too long. Steve liked Beatrice. She was caring in a tough way.

"I donna know. Two, maybe three years." Though smart, Beatrice spoke fluent Chicagoan. Heck, she had been a Chicago cop for 26 years, she had to get along with her squad mates. Beatrice had pulled the retirement pin several years ago and now spent her time walking her pampered dog Frankie and working on her house.

"Well, it's good to see you. How come we don't see you at Cera's, no more"? Jeez, she even had Steve lapsing into his makeshift Chicagoan. As a short timer, it didn't sound right. He did miss seeing her at coffee though. Beatrice was a talented abstract painter that Steve only found out about when he bid on one of her paintings at a Police Benevolent Association fund-raiser for an injured cop.

After he bought it, a steal at $600, she requested that he keep it a secret:

"Hey, can we keep it on the QT (confidential) that I am back to painting? It took me a long time to get back to where I feel confident that I'm making progress and I don't want these well-intentioned numbskulls to trip me up again."

Steve remembered how the coffee klatch had ruined her art gallery debut opening three years ago by spilling merlot wine all over an interested, well-heeled patron. Rick refused to apologize and then offered several freaking F-heimers. Beatrice, mortified, burst into tears and the showing was a bust. Literally. Rick next tripped stepping backwards and knocked over a limited-edition sculpture that the guys each chipped in $200 each and the sculpture now minus an ear also graced Steve's coop.

"You know, I'm just too busy to make it up there and the traffic is a bear from Park Ridge on." Beatrice looked both ways to make sure no one else was listening: "I'm happy to invite just you and Ann to my next showing at the Park Ridge Art Center. But remember, it's not an open invitation."

"That would be great. We'd love to come." Though Ann had made it clear that he was no longer permitted to single-handedly decorate their unit with art by someone like Beatrice who already had a decent pension and didn't need any financial help.

The group next attempted a discussion about who drank the most coffee. To Beatrice, it was no contest, cops did without question: "With all the double shifts we work, gotta be cops, no question about it." Ted, an over volunteered grandparent, was having none of it: "While I appreciate the effort you cops put in, your hours are nothing compared to a grandparent dealing with a grandchild with the croup. Besides, you, at least, get a good pension bump as a result of the extra hours." Ted knew, for two of his children were police officers. So, it went. The conversation flowed into who had the toughest working conditions. Ted, the construction worker, lyrically referred to the harsh winter winds off Lake Michigan. Beatrice countered with the endless hours of police work with sudden abject terror.

Lured by too many conversations at once, Steve was lulled into a daydreaming phase. All the conversations had an almost musical bent to them: True, there wasn't much listening going on, as usual, but everyone was happy, and they had all made it to the other side of A.C., after Covid.

Well, almost all. Steve and the others still had a hard time believing that Ralph had been taken away so quickly, just a couple of weeks ago. He was too young to have died from Covid. When Ralph had stopped showing up to coffee again, the guys figured he was just in one of his moods or just embarrassed over the Zoom Tango competition where he and Jackie never showed up. After a couple weeks, Theo went to Ralph's house, yet again, but when he pounded on the door, he found it was unlocked. Even though he had a bad feeling, Theo went inside. Ralph never left his door unlocked, after all this was Chicago. There was an odd echo when he called Ralph's name. Then in the bedroom, slumped against a king-sized bed that he shared with his books, was Ralph with Jackie the Roomba nestled next to him. There was an overpowering sick almost sweet smell and there were dried fluids on the floor from his body. Theo hurried over and felt for a pulse. There was none. Ralph wasn't old enough to die, he was only in his 60's, thought Theo. Damn shame. Because of the unusual way he found the body, with Jackie nestled next to Ralph, and the unlocked door, Theo decided to call the cops. The police came quickly, found nothing suspicious other than the open door, and to be careful, called in the coroner. Later tests revealed that Ralph died from Covid. After his first shot, Ralph decided not to get any booster shots because of the adverse effects he suffered. Well, death is a pretty adverse effect, too, Theo thought. Blaming himself, if only Theo had gotten Ralph to get the Covid booster or stopped by sooner. Survivor's guilt was all too common. It was an additional, permanent weight tied to the survivor's heart.

There was no funeral. Ralph, ever the High School Chemistry Teacher, had donated his body to science. Theo would have been too broken up to go, anyways. Theo's solution to the extreme, continuing guilt was to leave Ralph's chair permanently empty at coffee. It didn't make the weight of guilt any lighter but at least Theo felt he had done something. Staring at the empty chair at breakfast, Steve felt his mind continue to wander. Steve had already learned the hard way at coffee, not to sit in the memorializing vacant chair.

"Hey, Mr. Sleepy head, we were talking to you. Did you fall asleep with your eyes open again?" Boy, Theo was crispy.

Steve realized that they all were looking at him: "Nah, I was just trying to remember the last time we were all here at Batter Up? Must be my Sometimer's again. Sorry."

"We're just trying to figure out a date for our outdoor summer party." Theo felt someone had to take charge.

"Why the rush? Don't we have time til 10 pm to make a decision, when they close?"

Theo was not amused. When he was irritated, he frowned, and his eyebrows almost touched:

"What's that got to do with the price of tea in China?" Less a comment than a challenge. The tea comment meant Theo was fairly or unfairly irritated. Since Ralph's death, that feeling had become more common to Theo.

Steve couldn't resist though he should have: "Cause, it will take you that long to come up with a date."

Theo erupted: "Who do you think you are, Jesus Christ, Super-star?" (He only said that when he was really, really mad.) Patrons at other tables were staring at them. "Alright, this is what we are going to do for Mr. College Graduate. (He strung out the last 3 words almost like a curse and maybe it was.) WE are going to hold the party outdoors at my place on July 6 at 4pm. Potluck, of course. Is that good enough for everyone?" No was not going to be an acceptable answer, so they all said yes, and quickly took off- Steve included.

Steve was glad he hadn't taken the car. It was so refreshing to be on a bike with the wind at his back.

Steve found himself riding on the bike path along McCormick Blvd to Rita's house in West Rogers Park. It was about a 5-mile ride from the pancake house. It was a beautiful ride, and between the canopy of trees and the nearby Skokie River, it was about 10 degrees cooler than what he would have expected. He shouldn't set off Theo like that, Steve knew better. But those guys were way off on dismissing the electric bike revolution. By 2022, 12 percent of all bikes were electric, and that number was growing quickly. In use for several decades in China, some experts believed there were almost 200,000,000 Ebikes in use by their population. In the U.S., there were far fewer, but sales were increasing quickly too, with over 300,000 sold a year. It was a fast-changing world with the coming of electrified personal mobility.

Steve was looking forward to seeing both his daughters and their brood, but Mc Cormack was a direct bike path and Touhy was further and not as direct. Although he wasn't as tight with his daughters as Ann was, he was surprised at how pleased he was to be home. Chicago was now their home and had been since Ann pointed out her plain need, more of a hunger, of watching their grandchildren grow on a daily basis. Steve, now glad they had made the move, although the lack of parking, crime and the anemic performance of Chicago Bears was still a concern. Chicago still was a world class city, in spite of its troubles, of which there were many.

A little tired, Steve cheated and set his Ebike at a 3 level electric pedal assist. The bike sprung forward. Even now, he was still surprised how much quicker the bike was with the electric motor. What seemed to be instant torque, was amazing. It almost seemed to be an independent spirit, and he was just along for the ride, being carried to his daughter's. While the large 23-to-30-foot statues along the path, were almost a blur, and indeed some were better viewed that way, it was a beautiful, serene though windy, ride. Steve had been impressed by how much parkland and nature that was available in Chicago. Perhaps, in a larger gritty urban area like Chicago, people needed to be reminded that nature and quiet could be found there also. The quiet allowed him to hear his stomach rumbling so he decided to stop at Hogie and Sons sandwich joint. Hogie had retired as a corporate attorney without a definite plan as what to do next when his college aged sons suggested they open up a healthy sandwich takeout place that had the temerity to taste good. It sure did and Steve ordered his favorite: Dorn's Revenge on whole wheat. Apparently, Dorn was an opposing attorney who always gave Hogie heart burn in negotiations. The sandwich had roast turkey, onions, pickled peppers and brown mustard. It was spicy, real spicy. He had considered going to Eastern Pizza run by his good friends Frank and Sophia, but it was Saturday and Steve wondered if they were still closed til 11 am. Even though Eastern had the best crispy gyros in Chicago, his stomach was unwilling to risk the potential delay of gluttony, so Steve turned his bike into the lot at Hogie's.

Once hunger pains were satisfied; he jumped back on the trail. Steve was quicker than he thought. He was already there at his daughter Rita's on Morse Avenue. Rita's family lived in a 1940's brick colonial that barely had enough green space for her

4 active kids- the average Chicago home lot size being 23 by 123 feet. Their house was a little more than 3,000 square feet. Rita and her husband Saul were happy there, living as modern orthodox Jews in the center of the Jewish hood aka West Rogers Park.

It being a Saturday when Orthodox Jews did not drive, Steve expected to find her home and did:

"Well, hello there stranger, kids, Poppy's back!"

It being Saturday, the TV wasn't on, and at several looked up from their books probably Nancy Drew or the Berenstain Bears:

"Hey, Poppy good to see you- how was your trip?"
Asked Michael.

"Did you bring anything for your awesome granddaughter?" This was of course, Yael, who suffered from high levels of self-esteem, though she was pretty cool. Yael, the first child Steve thought her name which means mountain goat in Hebrew, was at times, too appropriate

Steve felt his heart melt in a good way, like how hot fudge inter-acts with vanilla ice cream. He was finally beginning to under-stand why Ann was usually powerless against the smiling faces of their grandchildren as in: "Can we have a treat now? Or can you take me shopping for some special new Shabbos clothes?" Yael, in particular, was a professional, in knowing how to work the Bubbe system.

Only Shira, Hebrew for song, was still buried or married to her book, and hadn't said anything yet. If books were a best friend, Shira had many friends. Her favorite hobby was the piano but it being the Sabbath, piano playing would have to wait. In the meantime, an endless supply of interesting books from the Skokie library were almost a full substitute.

"Gosh. they had grown so much…" Steve was reminded how much he and Ann had missed in the last 2 years. Thank God! More an exclamation then a belief by Steve. They all survived Covid with no long-term effects. Other families were not so lucky. Steve was pretty sure that they all had grown at least 6 inches in the several years they had been gone. But Steve's physical review was interrupted by the clear direction of the House Operations Manager, Rita:

"Is that any way to talk to your Poppy after not being with him for almost 2 years?"

His heart was home. Where it belonged.

9. Still Being Cooperative.

Meanwhile, at their Chicago home, Ann was re-introducing herself to their coop unit. A thick quarter inch of dust seemed to be present on every level surface. At least, their unit didn't smell too musty. Only a little musty, so she threw open the six tall casement crank open windows to get the unit re-acquainted with fresh air. It was a spacious, almost 1600 square feet unit, that because of the casement windows, looked bigger than it was. With the windows open, it felt that they were floating above the park and perhaps they were. It wasn't perfect- nothing from this era was after 100 years. The wiring was quirky and not all the outlets worked. Plumbing was an adventure, and it was challenging to make changes. Ann had plotted to somehow remove the annoying pea green bathroom wall tiles. But all the three contractors who advised her not to, and the concern raised by the self-appointed experts of the morning coffee club had merely put a delay in her plans. Inhabiting a 100-year-old building was like finding oneself occasionally trapped in the body of someone who was born in the 1920's. Emergency surgery on the fragile building was always a risk. It was like having an elderly parent, except this one was made of brick. But even with the original hardwood floors that reverberated every sound and everything else, it was still home.

Ann took a break for a handcrafted salad and then settled down to read. But her body needed more rest and she found herself waking at 4pm by the happy din from the gazebo.

Outside, Ann could see the Ladies of the Vine in full bloom with their sun hats and flowered dresses. Ann squinted and could see something dangling from the flagpole. Oh-Oh. This was not good. A closer examination revealed it was Steve's Batman boxer shorts. The ladies were welcoming them back and making a valid point at the same time. Word had obviously spread about their return and Steve had again left clothes in one of the communal washing machines downstairs. The ladies warned Steve some time ago about retrieving his wet clothes promptly. Yet, he had done it again, in spite of their past complaints about his careless actions with his unmentionables. Steve didn't do it on purpose but was absent-minded and believed his clothing, his dishes and the garbage would eventually find their way to their proper place. Typical slob, typical male. It was very annoying to everyone except Steve. Still, Ann was going to need to liberate her superhero's underpants for they were Steve's favorites. He said the Batman boxer shorts made him a superhero in and out of the bedroom. More perceptive, he said. Really. Whatever. Some boys never grow up. Anne grabbed a box of white wine to assist in negotiating the hostage's release.

"Hey Ann, so good to see you and your caped crusader. We heard noises from your unit. When is Steve returning from Gotham City?" asked Sima. Gotham City, being where Batman lived in the comics.

"Or is he hiding in his bat cave?" said Rose with a smile. "We've warned him repeatedly about leaving wet clothes in the laundry machines." Okay. So, they had finally gotten tired of picking up after him and they have been more than patient. But Steve was well known to be more than absent-minded on a good day and often forgot where he had left things.

What they didn't know because Steve hadn't told anyone, was he had Glaucoma, in addition to his Prostate Cancer and could no longer distinguish shapes in the dark basement. Still, this was not an acceptable excuse, especially when he hadn't told anyone at the building as to what was going on with his eyes. But Steve was proud and more honestly, scared. Steve knew that Glaucoma was no longer an automatic sentence of blindness that it was in the past. Between the special drops and high-tech surgery there was a good chance Steve could keep his vision. But as a writer, Steve wanted to see what he wrote and the throbbing pain in his eyes, especially at night, was like an ever-louder drum beat. Besides, how could he get by without being able to see Ann as the first thing in the morning and the last thing at night. But if there was ever a kind support group, it was here at the Gables. People leaned on each other here and would help a person stand up again to extent they could. Simply put, it was an extended family. These days, everyone needed all the help they could muster. So, Batman's loyal sidekick rescued Batman's underwear at a price of one box of white wine and her famous eggplant casserole, so that Batman's underpants could go back to being where they belonged: undercover.

10. The Losses Continue.

Yet the losses continued in the summer. Covid repeatedly marched through the country as an avenging angel. But avenging for what? Many patients died before family or friends knew they were sick. Mourners still gathered outside or over zoom to try and avoid causing yet another covid super spreader event. Others, like the Coffee Klatch tried to act as if the Pandemic was already in the rearview mirror. But it wasn't. Some people sat in close quarters inside without masking. So many others were just "Over it" and went back to their routines. Red States sued to get rid of mask mandates. A significant percentage of the population, about 30%, still hadn't gotten their vaccines and TV hosts were pushing bleach and home remedies as legitimate treatments. Somehow during an election year, even science had become politicized. People yelled they had the right to remain unvaccinated and that it was their body. But the right to remain unvaccinated, infected people who hadn't asked for it. Even more people died as a result. Needlessly. Steve found out Al who owned a bike shop, had died only when

Steve went to pick up his spare bike. The shop was locked up and the lights were off. A short-handwritten notice reported that Al had died two weeks ago from Covid and left the telephone number of how to pick up their bike from Al's son. God rest his soul, the note said. Steve called and found out that Al, who been overweight and prediabetic, had died quickly. "He thought he was safe because he ate healthy and didn't believe in the shots." The son explained, who now had deal with 60 bikes with some unknown owners and a handwritten inventory system. Tragic. Preventable.

So, Steve dutifully reported what had happened at coffee, the next day, thinking maybe, it was a teachable moment. It wasn't. Even though casualties included first Ralph and now Al.

"You don't know for a fact the vaccine would have saved him." Said Rick whose vaccination booster status Steve had always doubted. Now, Steve doubted it more.

"I did my part trying to get him to take vinegar every day- but he actually laughed, saying his probiotics would keep him safe." Theo opined.

"Omega Threes, that's the key!" Russ was always pushing fish, saying that as the descendant of a seafaring people, the Greeks, he knew the power of fish on the body and the mind. Russ called it, his Mediterranean Pharmaceutical Diet.

Stu counseled taking the nutritional supplements pushed by Dr. Oz who was also a candidate for the U.S. Senate. After all, it was on TV. While Stu was wise on most things, Steve had long ago stopped taking Stu's medical advice. Lately, Stu had been pushing some sort of brain regime that consisted of swallowing ground up apricot pits enhanced with meteorite dust. Really.

Steve did mostly what Ann, a retired Registered Nurse advised, apart from continuing to go to morning coffee. Ann thought that was still too risky, health-wise, and maybe it was. But Steve knew it was more emotionally unhealthy, not to go. Steve and Ann were otherwise- pretty dang careful. As grandparents, they had to be. Some of their grandkids were not yet able to be vaccinated because they were too young. So, Steve and Ann masked up religiously, tested for Covid often, restaurant meals were usually takeout only, and did not entertain inside their home. It was a drag, but their grandkids were worth it. They knew other grandparents who were even more vigilant.

Meanwhile, Steve had brought a problem to the brain trust to fix or more likely to break. Steve had not inherited much from his grandfather, so he was pleased when his cousin Jeff passed along their grandpa's sterling silver belt buckle with his initials W.G. short for William Greenberg on it. Even with eight years of post-High School education, Steve could not figure out how to tighten a belt with no holes in it. Maybe that's why it had a U.S. Patent Number 3020. Steve spent an hour trying to get it to work without success. Even Google and YouTube provided no answers. Humiliated and unwilling to risk yet another wardrobe malfunction as he had once with his Minneapolis Coffee Klatch (the infamous falling pants), Steve swallowed his pride and brought the unyielding buckle as a test to the group. If Fred had been there, he would have started with him but as a no show, Steve handed the challenge to Ted whom he believed to have the next highest clothing I.Q. Ted always wore decent high-priced duds that were always, always, neatly pressed. But even Ted's knowledge of sartorial splendor was not match for the resistant belt. Then Theo took a gander, but even with his pushing and pulling, he could get nowhere with the tricky belt. Finally, Rick grabbed the belt, pondered it for a minute, and switched where the belt buckle attached to the belt and snapped it in its proper place. Easy-Peasy. Humiliating, especially coming from a guy whose idea of fashion was to buy a new baseball cap to go with his old sweatpants. Steve tried to comfort his own bruised ego, by noting Rick was getting his master's in history, after Rick also quickly found the value of 100-year-old belt buckle on eBay. Somehow, that wasn't enough.

11. A Death.

Even as a recent transplant, Steve came to appreciate what a great city Chicago was. On the plus side, it had a great history, neighborhoods and parks. The sleek modern downtown skyscrapers appeared to pierce the clouds and slice the sky. Maybe, they really did. The Downtown even had great shopping, but to be honest, these days with the internet options who really needed that? Most of all, it had the inland sea of Lake Michigan which stretched forever beyond the horizon. On calm sky-blue days. Steve would see the boats bobbing their satisfaction in agreement. While on stormy days, it pounded the shore with its steel grey waves. In respect, the Native Americans called it large water or: "Michi Gami." The Native name eventually evolved to its current name: Lake Michigan. The names may have changed over time, but the Lake itself, remained constant in its ever-changing, powerful form. Steve liked that.

But even as a large world class city, Chicago had more than its fair share of world class problems, the most significant being crime. Whole sections of the west and south side were infested by crime and criminal elements that were spreading throughout the city. People were robbed outside their homes in broad daylight and carjackings were common, too common. Daily gratuitous violence was now expected by residents. Still the residents remained loyal to their hometown and tried to continue their daily lives.

Parking Paul still liked to hang out in Warren Park after the coffee and feed the squirrels. Paul felt a special kinship with the squirrels who spent most of their day, chasing after each other and trying to steal each other's food or possessions, typically a small twig. Kind of like life in the big city. Paul had a favorite bench along Pratt Avenue, and he could spend hours watching them play. On occasion, he would bring a small jar of peanut butter and serve it on a leaf, much like a religious offering. The largest squirrel that he nicknamed Skippy, would dart in and out, looking out both ways before snatching the tasty leaf. To Paul, Skippy looked like a smash and grab felon caught on camera. It was more fun to watch than a nature documentary on the Animal Planet channel.

It had been an interesting day at coffee, Paul thought as he dozed off. Sam, the retired electrical contractor and car collector, was reminding all present, of the dangers of smoking while painting. Never a good idea. Tom Bellicose, not the brightest painter, had just finished painting the floor with a thick oil-based paint when he decided to take a break and light a cigarette by the old furnace. Bad move. WHOOSH! The resulting arson investigation never definitively determined whether it was the paint fumes or furnace that was sparked by the cigarette lighter. In any case, Tom was not alive to answer any questions. The Arson Investigator, Sam's nephew, did say Tom looked pulverized. Clearly, not a pretty sight. Paul shuddered but not enough to really wake up. Theo had warned him about napping in public- it was too dangerous. Paul blew him off saying confidently that no one was going to bother him. He was wrong. CLANG, CLANG, CLANG. Paul felt the metal bench vibrate from something hitting it.

His eyes opened to a scraggly white teenager, about age 20, in a green fatigue army jacket, banging a thick bicycle chain and lock on the bench. In Chicago, youths, swinging bicycle chains, would lash on unsuspecting seniors from behind so they could then rob them. This punk apparently was trying the more direct frontal approach:

"Hey, old man-I'm hungry. Got some money to buy me breakfast at McDonald's?" McDonald's was on Western Avenue, a short bike distance away.

Paul was tired and not in the mood to be hassled:

"You hungry enough to get a job?" Paul had worked all his life, why couldn't they?

The would-be punk was not amused by this response. He quickly pulled out a large 6-inch switchblade from his pocket, opened it, picked at his cuticles leisurely, then said:

"Hey, my job is robbing old geezers like you. I know you got your wallet here. I saw you drive in. Hand it over!"

Paul stood up. Theo had advised them all to always give up the wallet without protest- politely-quickly. ALWAYS. It just wasn't worth it. Or maybe, in this case, it was. Paul wasn't in the mood to tolerate any creep taking his hard-earned cash:

"No, I don't think so. I made my own money; you can do the same. Get the Hell out of here and work for yours, too." Paul was tired of people telling him what to do. What gave this punk the right to push him around?

The feral punk looked around, saw no one, and then his right arm with the knife, suddenly darted twice, deep into Paul's abdomen. Paul felt the stabs but was surprised it didn't hurt more. The red stain grew like a glass of wine spilling on his tan shirt. His knees buckling, he fell to the ground, his final thought- feeling he was getting cold.

The Coffee Klatch somehow found out about the death of Paul when it was reported on the news. Violent death was all too commonplace in Chicago but did still drive the local TV news. Most of the coffee guys did show up at the outdoor funeral at Rosehill Cemetery. Rosehill Cemetery was a gem. Opened in 1864, Rosehill was a 330-acre cemetery (largest in Chicago) that held hundreds of Civil War Veterans including 12 Generals. It was a beautiful, quiet hilly area that attracted deer and visitors. As a Civil War buff, it was the perfect place for Paul to wait out eternity. No one had come from Paul's place of work. But the Coffee Klatch did. At least, the guys now knew his last name: Altman.

12. The Next Day.

The next day, the gang dealt with Paul's death, by how guys typically deal with tough subjects, by not talking about it. They know they should talk about it but were afraid to reveal too much of themselves. Violence didn't seem real until it hit your friends or family. Then, it was all too real. The Guy's Code would say that discussing feelings was weak and unmanly. Theo and Steve already knew this, being lucky enough to be educated over time by their better halves, i.e., their spouses. Most women just usually, instinctively, understood that people needed to grieve their losses and be given the time to heal to the extent they could.

But somehow that needed grieving hadn't happened with all the Covid deaths. There were just too many deaths, and they came about too quickly. Friends, coworkers, neighbors, parents, children, and spouses- the losses were whispered about, if at all. Maybe, the deaths happened too fast. Some survivors and family members just couldn't think about it- it was just too hard. Survivor's guilt? People felt guilty that they had survived, and their loved ones had not. Very understandable. So, people carried on, but with overwhelming grief just below the surface.

Beatrice walked in. She looked happy. They hadn't seen her since the pancake breakfast:

"Well, if it isn't the Brain Mush. Screw up any solutions lately? Looking kinda glum…"

Theo went right to it:

"Parking Paul died; his funeral was yesterday."

Beatrice's face fell, then said simply: "Covid?" Logical guess. People always assumed that now.

"No, he was murdered at Warren Park." The random, horrifying violence made it somehow worse.

"Wait, wasn't that the guy on the news, wasn't that Paul, that fed the squirrels?" Most cops didn't watch the news, they were all too familiar with violence in all its varieties. Yet as a retired cop, Beatrice felt she still had to get her daily "fix" by watching the TV news. Sometimes, now she got too much of it. They all did.

"Aw, ain't that a shame, he was one of the good ones." Beatrice was right. Paul was one of the good ones. He was, as people liked to say: "Real Chicago". But life moved on. Sort of.

The rest of them started talking about the violence problems in the city. Every day it seemed to come ever closer. People still went about their business but felt the cold sense of danger on the back of their neck. After Paul's death, their necks felt even colder. Most of them stayed inside their securely locked homes after dark. Theo, a notoriously light sleeper, listened to his police scanner every night. Theo reported his findings every morning, usually vague and ominous. Theo's lack of sleep didn't help his reporting any. But then as the unelected Mayor of Western Avenue, Theo had a duty to report:

"Busy night last night- cops in the district were constantly on the move. There must have been 3 shootings alone by the gang-bangers. Only 2 cops on duty to protect 30,000 people in our district!" Theo's belief that the district was understaffed, was a common refrain by residents. But it was true, too. Chicago was down by over 1,500 cops, city wide, since what Theo called the troubles, i.e., Covid and George Floyd's death and riots.

"Tis, a shame." Ted was sympathetic. His son Leo was a cop in Glenview, Illinois. Though it was a whole different police experience in the upscale suburbs there.

Several heads nodded in agreement.

But Beatrice had been busy. She had moved into her small bungalow in the suburb of Niles when her Condo Rules in the City would not allow a dog. The dog: Frankie, a Wiener Dog, had been a lifesaver during Covid. Men were too undependable except for one dangling thing, while Frankie and his Prostate was always happy to see her. They ate meals together, went on long walks and settled in to watch TV every night. Beatrice felt lucky to have such a stalwart partner during the long night that Covid had been. It would have been longer, had she not had her Frankie. Frankie was lucky too, to have landed such a good gig, after being up for adoption for several weeks at the rescue shelter.

Others, too, made significant changes to get through Covid. Home offices became "the real deal". Several friends had parents or adult children move into their homes. For example, Joe's daughter Jody moved home at age 33. Jody was a talented writer working on HER version of the great American novel. In HER case, it was an unusual adventure. It was a graphic novel about a butterfly who was flying across America. Jody's working title was: Mea Culpa/ Metamorphosis and she had been working on it for three years off and on. Mostly off. Back then, she had been able to financially support herself as a waitress at a high class, high buck steakhouse in downtown Minneapolis. When the restaurant closed during the quarantine, Jody after being invited by her parents, decided to hunker down in their basement. Like a lot of young adults, she really didn't have much of a choice when everything started shutting down. Jody couldn't afford the $4,000 a month apartment/art studio on just her income. Apart from the smell of herbal remedies, read marijuana, lazily floating around, Jody and her parents got along just fine. The herbal cure may have had something to do with that.

Still others tried to adopt new hobbies that people could do on their own or outside. Golf made a big comeback. Same for outdoor tennis. Plenty of social distancing there. Tim tried researching the family history using genealogical sites until he found out he may have been related to bank robbers who were alleged socialists. As a real estate developer, he wasn't sure which one was worse. Other friends were more exotic.

Ted took up psychic welding, which a few artsy people in the know, preferred calling Intrinsic sculpture. Huh? Ted believed the ancient spirits called to him and that would complete his sculptures. He did a spiritual map of the 12 tribes of Israel, made of heavy, really, heavy steel which he completed in less than a day. Steve was genuinely touched when Ted gave it to him at coffee one morning. Theo, on the other hand, was on a quest to grow olives in his backyard. So far, it had been a futile effort, and this was after unsuccessfully trying to grow pomegranates. Still, Theo was an optimist, and he would eventually find a crop, he felt it in his bones and corns for that matter. Maybe he would try pears next. Theo had read on the internet that they were a good source of Vitamin C and K.

Then there was Steve and his wife. Ann had her 3 book clubs that still met on zoom. She had also started jazzercise again on zoom. Not zooming enough, she signed up for 2 additional bible study courses on zoom although Steve teased her that they might cancel each other out. Steve also suggested some zoom dating so that the two of them could see more of each other.

Steve was doing a little legal work but still spent most of his time biking and writing. After his latest bike accident, he had plenty of time to catch up on his novel. The accident had been no one's fault but his own. With the streets still so empty, Steve felt he could blow stop signs with impunity. Steve figured he must have pissed off the car behind him by blowing through two of them and blocking the car from passing him. So rather than continue to honk at him, the car, a 2002 Buick Century gave his bike a little nudge, more like a kiss. The last thing Steve remembered was flying over his handlebars- thinking, this was not going to end well. It didn't. Steve landed on his shoulder with his thick, black, aerodynamic bike helmet cutting 2 of the tendons from his shoulder. He didn't remember anything except his beautiful $8000 carbon fiber bike was trashed, and he and his shoulder in a sling were now sitting in the car with his domestic supervisor. Ann, who was driving, was not happy. Seemingly, deservedly, so: "You could have been killed. You had a concussion and a torn Rotator Cuff. You are on Narcotics and won't be able to drive your car or ride your bike for 6 weeks."

Steve wanted to make a clever retort or at least a pithy comment, to reassure Ann that he still had his marbles. He still had something upstairs, otherwise he wouldn't hurt this much. Steve remembered that one of his friends, Carl, had told him that there were two kinds of bikers-those who have had bike accidents and those who are about to, but he felt pretty groggy and only said: "Aha." Apparently, some of those marbles had been moved about a bit, more than he thought. He wished he could remember the name of the friend who told him that, but he couldn't.

"You scared the daylights out of me. I had warned you about biking more carefully." Finished for the moment, Ann dried a tear on the right side of her face.

"Uh, huh." Steve thought he said. She was right. Usually was. They were home. It was lights out for Steve as soon as his head hit the pillow. Still felt like he was flying as he went under the bed covers.

That night, Steve continued flying but as a seagull not a bicycle. He was flying high under the influence of his pain medications. That Morphine really did the trick. It was a pleasant flight and he found himself swooping high and then low. That's how life was- it pushed a person down and then inexplicably lifted them back up again. No sense to it all. Even under the influence of the Morphine, Steve found himself asking questions. He found himself wondering how many more hits the city could take? He wondered how many hits he or Ann could take? According to Theo and his other friends- not too many. Some of Theo's long-time Chicago friends were bailing out of the city. Some retreated to the Chicago suburbs like Glencoe and Highland Park. Others made a total escape to Florida or Arizona. Maybe Steve and Ann should too. But Ann would never surrender her family especially her grandchildren voluntarily. Steve was kind of fond of the Big Lake and its ever-changing moods. Not all seagulls flew away.

So, several days later after he was off the narcotics, back on earth, Steve was again writing. He was working on his fourth or fifth novel depending on how a person counted. In his semi-retirement, Steve still wanted to do things that were meaningful but were more fun, too. He wanted to leave something behind. Legal paper shuffling was no longer not adequate. Stu, who knew about Steve's fanciful, literary fantasies, said Steve was- he was leaving behind- a pile of literary crap. Steve called it his "Literary Dump." But that didn't dissuade Steve from his work. Steve and his ego knew he wanted to create something that said: "I was here-I mattered." Egotistical? You bet. But it didn't make his version of the truth ring any less true. Or anymore. At least for him. We all have to live our own truths. Or not.

Steve secretly hoped his books would be a comfort to loved ones when he and Ann were on the other side of the grass. (Dead) Besides, he had a whole collection of characters from life and his imagination that just needed to be let out every now and then. Characters need fresh air, too. Better for their allergies. Yes, both real and unreal characters have health concerns, too. So anyways, he just kept on plugging along with his novels. It was amazing how much time his literary putzing could eat up during Covid and afterwards. At least in Chicago, he didn't have any yard work anymore.

Then, there were those who binged. On everything. Zooming was certainly more than a thing. (yes David C., the author is referring to you) Food, liquor, and Netflix were also abused by people. After all, they could catch the virus any day- no matter what they did or didn't do. Thus, no real point in moderation. Their weekly, if not daily, Amazon deliveries reflected that-after all, why wait? Ann and Steve had their occasional shopping slips. They all did.

13. The New Semi- Normal.

All in all, there was no new normal. Instead, daily life continued to lurch forward. Sometimes, 2 steps forward, 3 steps back. People who could- started moving forward. Slowly, inexorably. As people emerged from the state mandated quarantines, people found some things went back to normal while other things were unrecognizable, even when people tried to put on the most rose-colored glasses they could find or order from Amazon.

The first thing that was apparent was how few people ventured out at first. Usual bustling places could be seen as literal graveyards where the Grim Covid Reaper might find them, so many people held out going out until they felt safer. A few never did so, it was months or years before they resumed their daily lives. Downtowns were ghost towns with less than a quarter of pre-covid business activity. Rather than take the now returning public transportation, Steve again whizzed along on his Ebike, even on city streets. The electric pedal assist had him riding in only 4 weeks.

Then, all of sudden, feeling more confident from the Covid Vaccine, it seemed overnight that people rushed en masse into restaurants and bars usually without masks. For some, it had been months since they had seen their friends, for others, years. But things were not the same. People had not survived Covid equally. Some lost homes or jobs, others lost loved ones while a few seemed to prosper. Those lucky ones seemed to float above it all without much ill affect. They had gotten the vaccine first, gotten groceries delivered and even knew what remaining restaurants were offering take out. Some people just knew how to manage. Such as it always was- or wasn't.

But even they were subject to the nagging supply shortages. Some things were just not available, others had to be put on back order while factories waited for parts and employees to return. Steve had friends who waited well over a year for a new car or furniture.

On this day, Steve was going to deliver some unrequested Basil Pesto to his other daughter Jan who lived in Anderson-ville. Heck, it was on sale at Costco and more importantly, it was available. He was going to do this after coffee, and only AFTER taking the long way along Lake Michigan. He was trying to be more careful since the accident and had even installed a rear-view mirror on his bike. This way, he could see his fate in advance.

At coffee, people were still evaluating risk in deciding how often to show up. Some valued members were still not coming because of the continuing risks even after getting the Covid Booster Shots. Others, like Steve, figured the bigger risk for him was in not coming. For people like Theo, Ted and Steve, they needed daily interaction with people in person. Kind of like flowers need the Sun. People need real people nearby, not two dimensional substitutes. Zoom didn't cut it. But real-life people in person did.

After Ann, Lake Michigan remained Steve's best friend in Chicago. Steve needed to see the Lake frequently, so more than once a week he would bike to the Lake Front Trail. Like a good friend, the Lake was always available and seemed to intuitively know his moods. Steve had gotten to know his friend's moods because of what shade of blue the Lake was wearing that day. There was happy blue that was a rich blue color on calm days.

Then, there was steel grey blue, that reminded Steve of a thousand-yard stare. No point in trying to talk to the Lake then with the crashing waves. Steve wasn't the only Chicagoan with a personal relationship with the Lake. Most just didn't talk or dream about it.

Now Jan and her husband Ray had gotten through Covid pretty well, and their 3 kids were happy and healthy. That's what counted and they knew that. Jan and Ray were pretty savvy. Steve was impressed by how quickly all their adult kids were able to pivot when they had needed to during the height of the crisis. Knowing when to zig and when to zag. Taking necessary precautions, taking reasonable chances-every day for young parents was a master class in risk analysis. As in, is it safe enough to take the kids to an outdoor birthday party? (Yes) Or is it ok to take the oldest to the indoor Shedd Aquarium? (No) All in all, their adult children were all pretty good on dancing on the head of a pin. They usually didn't fall off.

Steve and Ann felt fortunate.

Steve knocked on the door, tentatively. Jan was not home. She was usually happy to see them, but with a life, that like most young parents was spinning almost out of control, but not always. When that happened, it was a stone on Ann's heart. Not so much for Steve. He just wasn't wired that way. Most guys weren't. No one was home so he left the Pesto on the porch with a note. Hope she enjoyed it. Lord knows, she and Ray earned it every day and then some.

Steve did not feel as fortunate after leaving Jan's place on his way to his other daughter Rita's. He felt every time he biked, he was taking his life out of his hands and placing it into the Gods of the Potholes. (Yes, that prayer was a necessary thing in cities like Chicago.) Every 30 feet or so, there was a pothole, significant bump or piece of trash. It was like a major defensive perimeter set up in a third world country to prevent a person from getting anywhere. It was especially dangerous for bikers. Besides the general lack of civility on the road and those cars that seemed to chase bikes, the roads and sidewalks were equally unwelcoming. For DECADES, the City of Chicago had not maintained their streets and sidewalks. Steve complained several times to his Alderman who said there was nothing that could be done because there were "Budgetary Constraints." The only thing that didn't suffer from budget constraints was corruption. It was deeply entrenched, and its rot affected everything. The city wasn't left enough money to even replace its missing street signs. Steve's friends had warned him about the "Chicago Way" when they moved down there. At least corruption was fully funded. It felt more like an unfair tax, an extra 10 to 15% cost to everything is what Steve now figured. In the hopes of educating them before the move, one of his friends, Jerry gave them the excellent book: "Boss" by Mike Royko written in 1971. Still true today. It is a deeply funny, true book about the reign of Mayor Richard Daley, the Elder. (Yes, Chicago had a King) Some Chicagoans argued that at least under Daley Senior, the city worked. Now the city was comatose, and the cancer of corruption, poverty and gang violence continued to feast on what was left of the body. So, everyone suffered. So sad. So predictable. So Chicago.

Back to the lake trail, pedal assist level set at 2, and on to Rita's house. The Lake was pretty calm today, more blue than grey and there wasn't much wind blowing. Good biking weather. While he was biking at a pretty good clip 13 MPH with only a minimal assist from the ebike's motor. Still at times, he felt too old and more importantly too slow for the impatient and apparently immortal speed demons that would whiz by him without any thought or any notice. Ann was even more legitimately worried about some biker crashing into Steve without warning. Even with warning, it wouldn't be much better. But living every day is a risk, Steve figured. The key to enjoying life is to find the risks that were acceptable and meaningful. For now, biking sure was for Steve.

Steve took Ridge all the way to Pratt Avenue and then hung a left. Pratt had a bike lane and he made quick work- riding down to California Avenue. Before he or his bike knew it, he was there at his younger daughter's house. He spied through the front living room window. All there. Looked peaceful. Looks could be deceiving.

Steve had vegan chocolate chips for their daughter Yael who was a gifted baker at age 12. Not as gifted at cleaning up. The younger daughter Shira had her head in a book as usual. She loved to read and see where a book would take her. She was going to go places. Michael which means Gift from God- was 8, rambunctious and Steve's secret football watching partner. After all, the Chicago Bears needed all the help they could get. Mike was doing something with Legos and only later would he practice his Judo.

Rita was home holding the youngest, Kayla, 5 years old. Kayla looked like an extension to Rita's arm. It was where Kayla usually was, and Rita was an exhausted younger mom with a colicky child. Rita did not complain, she never did. She was happy to see him:

"Kids-Poppy is here." No response. Rita tried again-That was thing about Rita, she never stopped trying either: "Anyone who wants morning snack, say hello to their Poppy!"

That elicited more of a response, almost a groan/salutation from the kids: "Hello, Poppy…" The Y in poppy trailed off. Steve wondered how they would greet him as a teenager. Still, Steve would take whatever he could get. Most grandparents did. The kids went back to what they were doing.

Steve tried bringing up what he considered a fascinating piece of family history:

"Guess who Poppy is wearing today?" Yep, Steve was wearing the belt the coffee guys had rescued. Yael rolled her eyes. As the oldest child, she often set the tone.

"W.G., who was he?" Steve asked.

"William Greenberg-your grandfather." Moaned Yael. which in Hebrew also means God's Strength. She had seen the belt before. A lot. Too much. Right now, Steve was thinking her name's secondary reference to Mountain Goat was more appropriate. Still, he tried again:

"Correct. Glad you remembered. Anybody up for a board game or football outside?" Not much enthusiasm. Only Mike was willing to play football after he finished building what he called his Lego Control Center. Steve didn't have a clue as to what that was. The girls did not deign an answer. After all, Steve was a member of the weaker sex. Fair enough. The kids were just beginning to get out of the Covid Malaise. For months because of Covid concerns, the kids had been restricted to playing in the front yard or in the house. Steve and Ann were making a concerted effort to get them out more, now that vaccines had been expanded to children under the age of 12 and the kids had their shots.

He gave up trying to be an activities director and made some instant espresso coffee in the microwave. Steve then plopped down on the couch next to his daughter and Kayla.

"How's it going?" Steve asked. Probably asked that question too much. But he cared about his daughter and worried about her and the kids a lot. Probably did that too much also, especially since Covid. Rita successfully suppressed a sigh.

"It's going. Seriously Dad, you don't need to worry." Problem was- Steve thought he did.

He next looked out the front window:

"Looks like they finally painted the speed bump." Pretty observant of him. To prevent drivers from taking shortcuts, to avoid the terminally congested Touhy Avenue, Steve had even threatened to run for City Council to get the bump built.

"Michael. Will you take your Poppy out to play now?" She wasn't having any of it. She was right. Steve needed to go and do something. Often, it felt like the grandkids were babysitting him. Steve did feel better just being in their presence. He had never had this much anxiety before Covid. Ann joked that he needed to cut down to 6 cups of coffee a day. But between the restless nights and unfilled days, the anxiety shouldn't have been surprising. Everyone was more jittery. Had to be. No one knew what was coming around the corner next. Steve thought by now there should be a legal limit as to how many corners a person had to worry about.

As if the epidemic wasn't enough, there was all the nuttiness coming every day out of Washington D.C. While the 2016

Presidential Election was contentious, matters had only gotten worse since President Trump took office. Every day brought a new scandal or fight. While political divisions came from both sides, the new President seemed to relish his role as the Divider in Chief. Anger, Grievance, Fault were always in play. This was more than a recipe for disaster, it turned into a certainty when disaster hit in the form of the Pandemic. Just when society needed unity, the President preached division. Rather than tell the country that they were all in it together- after first minimizing the danger, the President punted and said essentially everyone, and every state was on their own.

Then as if there wasn't enough pent-up anxiety and anger- there was the death of George Floyd on May 23,, 2020. While mostly peaceful demonstrations against racism erupted throughout the country, there was rioting in a number of cities including Minneapolis and Portland. Rather than appeal for calm, President Trump instead walked to Lafayette Park to make a point, after peaceful protesters were forcibly removed. The country seethed and it was as if the nation needed group therapy. Every day, every week was another crisis. (See Timeline) As a country, Americans sunk further into a societal abyss.

While the Fall 2020 Federal Election that chose President Biden, should have been a soothing salve, but as history showed, the soon to be former President Trump refused to accept the results.

January 6th Riot was a last gasp by those who could not accept the results. Only later did it become clear how close the Nation came to a coup d'état, happening in plain view. It wasn't for lack of trying.

But the vast majority of people found a way to get through that horrible year of 2020. It wasn't easy. No wonder, people were exhausted. For those keeping score of that grueling, historic year 2020, see Timeline at the end of the book.

Still while people had to hunker down during the worst of it during the quarantine, others found ways to maintain the lifelines of friends and family. People did not have to go through this Plague alone. Mostly, they didn't. For not being alone, and in having each other- Steve and Ann were extremely grateful.

Today, Steve was reminded of that again. The kids were comforting. Calming. They were getting through this thing, whatever it was. Steve would, too. He followed his grandson outside to play.

14. Just Walk Away.

Ann resumed going to her in person exercise and book clubs and distinguished role as Bubbe. Steve? Still drifting a bit. Zoom was getting to be a drag and he needed some more activity. Jan suggested meetup groups maybe hiking. Not a bad idea.

Meetup Groups were a thing that exploded in use during the Pandemic. Essentially, it was an internet solution as to how to make new friends with common interests. During the pandemic, people would search the groups and find people with similar interests in a nearby location. His daughter Jan, who was knowledgeable in such things, suggested joining several, and then ditch the ones that had "weirdos" as she put it. Steve had found what he thought would be a mellow hiking group. It was anything but. Its leader Rob was a unique character in a good way. Rob, short, stout in his 70's, still threw around, a twenty-pound kettle weight. He had started his own hiking group when he was requested not to return to another. This was after Rob had been arrested at a Bears game for mouthing off to Chicago's Finest, i.e. Da Police. Rob being Rob, had shrugged his shoulders, moved on and founded his own hiking group. A variation of changing lemons into lemonade. His group hiked several different trails on different days. Each day attracted different people and had a distinct personality. Steve valued Rob and enjoyed the group. Participants rambled in and out. Hikers included retirees, refugees from Corporate America and loners who had not found their tribe yet. Some of the younger walkers came once and were never seen again. Others found it becoming an important part of their life. Bill found that he did not have to slowly melt inside a large Bank. His partner Sue, a Chief Financial Officer discovered her artistic soul after an unplanned retirement. Sue had just scheduled her first art showing at the Tin Roof Club, a well-known northside neighborhood bar.

Surprisingly, the Chicago Park District had a large and very well-developed trail system. The Park Reserves were magnificent at this time of year in the Fall. The trees erupted in an explosion of red and orange leaves. The wide variety of animals that inhabited the rivers and marshes seemed to appreciate what they had. There were squirrels, ducks, beavers, and so many happy animals that Steve sometimes believed he had stepped into a live children's book. There were even deer that apparently never drank caffeinated coffee for they appeared to have lost their fear of Man. The deer were totally chill in a good way. The walks were simply grand.

Rob and Steve would play Historical Jeopardy. One would first give the question and the other would have to supply the answer. For example, who was Felix Dzerzhinsky? Answer: Founder of the Cheka, a predecessor of the Soviet KGB Spy Agency.

But that is how you build a new life. In bits and pieces. On this particular day, Steve and Rob were arguing (both would say it was merely a vigorous discussion but whatever…) as to whether the dissolution of the USSR was the biggest disaster in the last 100 years for Russia. Steve said no, while Rob maintained it was, agreeing with Putin. (Steve wasn't really sure that Rob really believed that, but Rob did firmly believe in being contrary as a way to invigorate the discussions.) Both talked better than they listened. But that's how it is for old friends or in this case, new intense friends. Before they realized it, they had already finished the six-mile hike and were back in the parking lot. Bill and

Sue suggested going out for lunch and proposed Flounder's, a seafood joint on Dempster Avenue. But Steve had to beg off today for he had already agreed to have Shabbos lunch with Rita.

Ann was probably already there. She was always on time. Ann was good that way- she was considerate of others and their time. Steve? Not so much. Oh, he meant well and tried hard to be on time, but it seemed his internal clock was always running 15 to 30 minutes late. Saul was even later, walking in with red cheeks that showed his real physical effort not to be the last one there.

They gathered at the oak table first used by Steve's grandmother, who would have been pleased to know that her progeny still gathered there for festive occasions. Many happy occasions were spent there. The kids had set the table and that probably explained why some place settings had an extra fork or were missing a spoon. Quality control could be an issue with some of the kids in charge, but they were happy and that's what mattered. Shira with her interest in music, was the most disciplined in setting the table properly. With Michael, Steve was lucky to get a spoon. Yael was beginning to pay attention to style and was placing the cloth napkins in the empty water glasses. It was good to see them all together working almost cooperatively. These kids were going to do great things. So their Bubbe said. Often. Maybe, they already were. Rita and Saul were good parents. Stealing a glance at Ann's beaming face, Steve was reminded again why they had come back so quickly. Spending time with family was worth it. Almost always.

15. Meet Up to Break up.

Rob said his different hiking groups had different personali-
ties. Steve didn't understand why, but it was so. Maybe it was
because the weekday hikes attracted different hikers than the
weekend. Steve would have assumed that the weekday groups,
with a higher percentage of the self-employed and retirees,
would be more chill but that wasn't the case. These weekday
warriors had goals and places to be. They almost never went
out for coffee or lunch.

The weekend hikers were different. They walked slower and
were usually available for coffee or brunch. This was important
to Steve because as a newcomer, he was still trying to develop
a list of places to hang out and eat. It made Steve feel more
connected to his new adopted hometown. He needed to find
his own "hole in the walls." The Pandemic had decimated the
number of restaurants, but Chicago still had a wide variety of
superb ethic joints. The remaining hot dog stands, and breakfast diners were getting harder to find. The Saturday walks were
Steve's favorite.

Steve did have to learn how to modulate his political beliefs on the walks and meals. People were not hiking to hear Steve regurgitate what he had heard that day on MSNBC. They would respond with what Tucker Carlson had told them the night before on Fox. Between the stress from the Pandemic and the continued political divisions, most people had locked themselves into their own information silos. It was far easier to argue than to really listen. It took Steve a long while to leave the political discourse, as important as it was, at home, and just enjoy the walk. But he did. Usually.

16. Simple Courage of Everyday Life.

Even with the widespread availability of vaccines, there were still heavy losses of life. People lost partners, parents, grand-parents, friends, coworkers and children. There was no rhyme or reason to the losses, but the Pandemic seemed centered around those over the age of 65 or with pre-existing conditions. Often, there was not time to even say their farewells before people succumbed to Covid. Even funerals seemed different and distant. Many burials were held on zoom or outside. It was simply too hard for many people to talk about. Slowly, people withdrew into themselves.

There were those who seemed better able to withstand the fierce winds of the furies. They seemed genetically endowed to rise to the occasion. They called their friends over the phone, got takeout meals for their children and met their friends for walks in the park.

The Ladies of the Vine held daily court in the Gazebo, offering cheer, wine and snacks to their neighbors. They kept track of how well residents were doing and contacting those who hadn't been heard from. It was important work and Steve often heard the laughter before he saw them from his second-floor window. Steve and Ann often joined them, knowing all were welcome.

Today, people at the gazebo were looking ahead to a day when Covid was in the past or at least manageable. The Ladies were planning a trip abroad and were trying to choose between an all-inclusive resort in Mexico versus a trip to Rome. Time wouldn't wait and neither would they. After a highly spirited discussion, all-inclusive with wine- won out. The Pope would have to wait. Besides, as everyone agreed, Italian wines were overrated and too expensive. So was Pessimism.

17. Coffee Sometimes Falls Flat.

The thing about daily Coffee Klatches was there was never a guarantee as to how many guys would show; even if they said they were coming. Some days there would be eight, other days it might only be two due to the luck of the draw. Guys were like that. Something could always come up. Like a last-minute babysitting gig or helping one of the kids getting their car repaired. There was always something.

In the group that met at Cera's, the regulars were Ted, Steve, Rick, and usually Russ, if it wasn't his day off, and Theo, of course. Theo was their North Star and was constant. Who wouldn't want to follow a Star? He had started the group, soon after selling his mini-mart and was still responsible for it. That was almost 20 years ago. Theo had also recruited all of the regulars and took a proprietary interest in how they were all doing. He had recruited Steve to their table after Steve started showing up at a now long closed diner. Steve had been checking out diners after moving to Chicago and pretty much abandoning (so, it seemed to them) his Minneapolis Coffee Klatch. While Steve still stopped by when he was in town, it wasn't the same. In his own defense, Steve felt he had to keep on moving forward and his Minneapolis club was in his rear-view mirror. But that's just how guys are. Here today and gone tomorrow.

That's how many of the "Floater's" were- they'd come by a couple times and find both the coffee and the group were not to their liking. Sometimes, the coffee and conversation was too strong, sometimes it was too weak. In this age of ever present, message echo chambers, many people, guys especially, only wanted to hang out with members of their own information silo. Team loyalty, Steve guessed.

Steve did notice that the loyalty pledge was not as strong in Ann's groups and that women could have civil discussions on politics. Not always, but usually. Ann believed this was due to the fact that women were more emotionally advanced and less aggressive than the weaker sex- the male species. Steve was inclined to agree. So, to keep things moving in a positive direc-tion in their coffee group, both Steve and Theo tried to avoid bringing up politics. But occasionally, Steve was sorely tempted to do so, especially when his coffee was cold and he could hear Fox News in the background. Maybe that's why Ann wouldn't let them subscribe to Cable TV in Chicago. She was concerned that they both, Ok well Steve, might overdose on MSNBC and CNN. But at morning coffee usually, both the coffee and discussion were at the right temperature thanks to Theo. Steve knew the outside world was still too cold as it was.

18. Burnt Toast Lodge.

The Kosher Kids had a week off from school due to the holidays. Their Dad still had to work so Steve thought it was a perfect time for a family adventure. Ann quickly signed on and they negotiated with their mother, who knew better, as to what was realistically achievable. Grandparents were not bound to such minor details. After first suggesting a mad dash to Walt Disney World in Florida on a cheaper 2 am flight, Bubbe and Poppy settled for a quick, still expensive enough, overnight to the Las Vegas of the kiddie world-the Wisconsin Dells. The Dells prided itself on being the waterpark capitol of the world. Tourists have been going there since the 1800's to enjoy the rough sandstone features that erupt out of the water. More importantly, at about 200 miles away from Chicago, it was certainly doable by van.

The next question to be answered was where to stay. With choices as varied as Noah's Ark to Mt. Olympus, they needed a place where they could prepare meals in their rooms (that whole Kosher thing going on) and participate in as many activities as possible, that respected their rules of decorum. (So swimming itself was out.)

After Steve and Ann cut down the number of resorts down to two finalists, Ann suggested that they leave the final decision to the kids to get even more buy in to the trip from them. On Sunday night they had the final meeting to determine which one to choose. The first option was the Bear Grease Lodge: It had decorated bear caves, microwave, fridge and offered virtual reality options that were pretty nifty that included a gold mining experience. Steve especially liked their menu that included Bear Claws donuts that he could have with his early coffee. The girls, being aspiring vegetarians, wanted nothing to do with bear grease so the Burnt Toast Lodge was the clear winner. Burnt Toast had a microwave and fridge required for self-catering that the family was required to do so that they could keep Kosher. Moreover, the lodge offered a bowling alley, indoor miniature golf, climbing wall, pinball arcade and gave each Toasty (yep, that's what they called them) under the age of 12, a free pair of toasty ear muffs to wear on their head.

The following Monday they were off. Rita, Yael, Shira, Michael, Kayla, Ann and Steve the self-designated driver. Saul, Rita's husband, had wisely decided to stay at home and work. It was grand getting out on the road again. The kids had not been outside of Chicago for close to 2 years, thanks to Covid. Steve worried that they had lost their sense of adventure. Steve took an exaggerated sniff: "Smell that kids? That's the smell of the open road!" Steve thought he was more excited than anyone.

"Yew, Poppy! It smells like one of Michael's stink bombs!" declared Yael. At age 10, Michael took fierce pleasure in the release of his own personal noxious fumes anytime his family was in a confined area. No one else did, though today Michel's colon was innocent: "That's a feedlot. It's used for cow production" Steve said confidently. He wondered if the kids knew how much pollution was caused by cows belching each year. Though not sure, Steve thought it was around 15 percent of greenhouse gas emissions annually.

"That's gross." said Yael, and Shira nodded her head vigorously. As the younger sister, Shira was supportive to her superior. Not always. So far, the trip was going pretty well. They had left only 1 hour later than they had planned. But no one with kids could realistically plan on being on time, especially on vacation. There was always time for one more battle royale before leaving yet. Maybe that's why so many families relied instead on staycations.

But kids' eyes need actual miles on the road to expand their vision, especially if they've been locked up for several years because of the Pandemic. Steve had always loved these road trips where the kids could let their guard down and let the adults peek inside. Sometimes but not usually.

But most of all, what Ann and Steve loved most were the treasured memories they created on the trip. They already had plenty. Kayla even went to sleep that night with her free "Toasty" earmuffs on.

The next day the kids were up earlier than the grandparents thought was possible. It wasn't even 7 am but the "Toasties" were already dressed and ready to be toasted, even the youngest Kayla. While it was Kiddie Las Vegas, most of the attractions did not open til 8 am so there was plenty of time for breakfast which in this case, meant scrambled eggs made on a Kosher personal pizza cooker. Then, after prayers and teeth brushing, it was already time for some wake-up bowling. The kids of course had drawn straws and Shira had won. Bowling at kiddy convention center is not exactly what one would expect but to the already caffeinated kids, thanks to Koshure chocolate cocoa, they were ready for some action! The miniature bowling lanes looked normal enough and the pint-sized bowling balls felt heavy enough, but when Rita tried to show them, the proper technique, the ball did not bounce and glide towards the bowling pins but instead landed with a THUNK like a frozen turkey that had fallen out of a grocery bag. The adults later surmised that the "bowling alley" was merely wood colored linoleum glued on top of the concrete floor. No matter. The kids were still charged up and having fun. While Michael assumed in typical male fashion that the Boys Team was ahead, the computerized score and Yael repeatedly informed him otherwise which meant the Boys Team was going to do the dishes that night. As a consolation prize, Michael got to choose the next activity and in the hopes of tormenting his sisters, he chose the most dangerous activity available: rock climbing.

The 30-foot climbing wall was located next to the wave pool. It looked fairly realistic and to Steve it looked like a plastic idealized version of the cliffs that Hwy 61 North of Duluth travels through- rocky and rugged. There was experienced teenage staff who wore t-shirts emblazoned with the words: Toasty Guide. Although Michael was surprised, Yael wanted to be the first. The instructor placed the safety harness on her and taught her how to grasp the rope. He then demonstrated how to start climbing up the "rocks". Yael scampered up and down so quickly, Steve barely had time to take a photo. Maybe her parents were onto something when they named her Yael. (i.e. the mountain goat) Next, it was Shira's turn, and although tentative at first, she went up and down like a champion. That left Michael who seemed to defy gravity running up the rope then sliding down as a spelunker would. Both ladies begged off and Steve should have, but ultimately was shamed into it.

Steve should have known better and after 45 minutes, they all knew better after the Burnt Toast Rescue Team carefully lowered him to the ground. Steve thought he had finally conquered his fear of heights when he climbed up. But when he looked down, the people looked so small and the padded floor still looked ominous. Though Steve was embarrassed to show what a scaredy-cat he was in front of his family, his legs would not move. The Rescue Squad tried to make him feel better by letting him know that Steve was not the first grandfather they had to rescue that week. Steve did not feel better until the Boys Team was victorious in the 3D Dino-Saucer competition. Before they knew it, it was time for dinner which they made in their Kosher plug-in panini machine. Each child made their own grilled cheese with veggies, part of Rita's healthy no veggie, no dessert plan. Ann and Steve were still astounded by how much less crap their children fed their kids. No pop, sugared drinks, food coloring or candy bars on their watch. The lack of preservatives and food coloring didn't seem to bother them much, and was hopefully setting them all on a healthy life style. While Steve supported their efforts for the most part, he drew the line at cutting Velveeta which was the lunch of champions.

After a change for bedtime, they all shuffled off to the Burnt Toast Lodge Story Hour at the super-sized fireplace. Though Ann rightfully wondered about the wisdom of telling ghost stories right before bed in front of a roaring fire, the simple stories told to a large, enraptured audience, was a highlight of their trip. Such is how lifetime memories are created and remembered.

19. The Neighs Have it.

It was their daughter Jan's idea to be Fall election judges. "It'll be fun." the text said. "We even get paid $265 for the day." The text neglected to mention that day of election work was from 5 am to 10 pm and the additional 6 hours of unpaid required on-line computer training. There was also an obligatory, 117-page election training manual to study. The "Opportunity" worked out to be a minimum of 23 hours or a little more than $10 per hour. It was less than Chicago's minimum hourly wage. Yuck. Still, it was a chance to spend more than 16 hours of almost face time with their daughter. They planned on texting and facetiming that day their shared experience in democracy-Chicago Style. Steve had originally been assigned to a different city school which like all other schools were closed. That way, the schools could serve as election sites.

November 8th, 5 am was cold and dark. Real dark, as if night was giving them a cold shoulder and perhaps it was. Ann was already tired, and Steve could not stop yawning. They had driven the two short blocks to Rogers Park School and waited patiently at the front door. Perhaps too patiently, for Steve found himself nodding off again. How they were going to get through the day, Steve didn't know. Right now, he didn't care.

Rogers Park Elementary School was built in the 1920's. It was a solid building, nothing fancy, but it was built with care by crafts- men who made $2 a day when it was built.

After a few minutes of waiting, the security guard let them in. Both Ann and Steve were carrying their own bags of food and books to get through the day. Ann brought books from 2 of her book clubs in addition to a healthy salad. Steve in addition to bringing a hot water maker just in case, also brought his small plug-in panini machine. Purchased for $9.99 at Walmart, it made perfect grill cheese sandwiches every time. Steve didn't know how it did that, all he cared about, is that it worked. He used it at least once a week. Twice a week if he was lucky. Steve thought it should be awarded the Nobel World Peace Cheese Prize.

The polls were open from 6 am to 7 pm. There was a lot of work to do, in advance, to get ready. Election booths had to be assembled, machines tested, voting forms distributed, and required Election Notices had to be posted. As rookies, Ann and Steve were assigned some of the grunt work but in most cases, it was quicker for the more experienced Election Judges to simply do the work. There was also a myriad of other official papers that had to be signed by each Judge attesting to the fact that the procedures and security precautions had been followed. Hey, it was Chicago, after all. Ann managed to look busy and official, even if she wasn't, while Steve made lineup changes for his Pink Flamingo Fantasy League Football Team. Even with a Covid mask on, Ann managed to look more professional. By this time, many people had given up wearing masks in public, but Steve and Ann continued to do so -better safe than sorry.

Before they knew it was already 6 am and the polls were open. There weren't many voters until 7am but then there was a steady stream of voters coming in early to vote before going on to work. While the Election Workers had prepared the best they could, there were a number of snafus that delayed voting. First, was the issue of voters trying to vote in the wrong precinct. This was not surprising because precinct boundaries had changed as a result of Chicago's declining population in the recent census.

Fewer Precincts were needed. Then, there was the issue of the markers. In an infinite lack of wisdom, the election powers that be, required that all precincts were provided only black markers that bled through the ballots. That problem was easily solved by Steve and Ann giving a number of black pens that they had in their bags. The next problem was the scanner machine that collected the ballots – jamming like an errant teenager because it felt like it. Eventually, they all learned to treat the machine like a belligerent teenager- just let it take its time.

Ann heard a ping and saw Jan had texted them: How's it going? Followed by a wagging dog emoji. Ann thought for a moment then texted back: Great, seen any friends so far? Ann shook her head, why did she ALWAYS have to do that with her daughter? It was only going to make Jan mad. Understandable response, but someday Jan might understand, that a mother can never stop constantly taking their children's emotional temperature whether kids needed it or not. Jan did not respond then finally: 167 voters so far, how about you?" Ann asked Steve what the numbers were, who by this point had been demoted to manning the voting scanner. On the other hand, he did get to hand out the vaunted red "I voted" stickers. Both Steve and Ann loved to vote and never took that right for granted.

"119" Steve announced unhappily. He was competitive and Jan had a strong lead already. Steve's only hope was that the Rabbis would direct their parishioners to get out and vote after the evening prayers. The morning rush of voters was over but there were still 12 long hours to go. The fun paid opportunity had long ago turned into a long-term sentence.

They heard from Jan again in the afternoon. She was dragging too: "Exhausted. Ran into three neighbors by 2 pm." Ann and Steve were tired, too. In fact, they had been tired all day. They were moving slower as if they were wearing some sort of invisible weighted clothing that weighed them down. Then again, Ann and Steve were two of the oldest Election Judges.

There was some excitement in the afternoon when attorneys from the State's Election Integrity Unit showed up unannounced. Steve picked them out right away after he saw the young, white, earnest attorneys in trench coats even though there was little chance of rain that day. While Steve and all the Election Judges had been warned they might pop in to monitor the election, Steve still made them produce their identification badges. Steve wished he had a badge to flash also.

By 6 pm, both Steve and Ann were beyond exhausted, almost comatose. Both were only talking, more like sleep mumbling when asked a direct question. They had long run out of their food and even the free pizza delivered by the local Alderperson had long disappeared. Steve began to consider contacting the International Red Cross for violations of The Geneva Convention against the torture of prisoners. At 8 pm Ann made a prison break: "Steve, I'm taking the car and going home. I can't take this anymore."

Steve tried to be sympathetic but couldn't quite pull it off, after all they were supposed to be in this together: "That's deserting your post! You won't get paid."

Given the fact Ann had been up since 4 am and had already worked for 15 straight hours, Ann had a logical response given the circumstances: "I don't care."

Steve pondered for a minute: "Tell you what. Let me drive you home and come back." To be truthful, Steve wasn't sure Ann was safe to drive after so many hours. Ann was wonderful but was a highly tuned, fine machine and right now, her life battery was flat lined. So was Steve's. His body moved in short robotic movements when it came time to finally disassemble the voting machines. He received a final text from Jan at 930 pm with a final vote count of 547. With only 399 voters, their precinct had lost. The Rabbis had not come through. While the final numbers didn't really matter, Steve felt oddly disappointed. He finally got home at 1030 pm after being up for 18 and ½ straight hours. It took them and their daughter Jan, 3 days to recover. No one ever said Democracy was easy. But no one ever told them, it would entail so much paperwork.

20. The Best Hike is the Current Hike.

The Kosher Kids were out of school and surprisingly, so was Raisa, who was Jan's daughter, and was the same age as Shira. It was a good day for a hike and Rita readily agreed to it. This was important because only Rita's minivan, 2020 Honda Odyssey, had enough room for everyone. While Steve appreciated its functionality, he was not inclined to believe its name alone made commuting more exciting. To be fair, Steve also didn't believe their SUV, a Toyota Highlander, made Ann and Steve, any more Scottish.

Still, it was a rare opportunity to get the cousins together, and as paid-up grandparents, Ann and Steve wanted to create memories and encourage connections. Rita the tour guide and driver was all in favor. As long as they hiked at least 2 miles (all right, only 1 mile), Poppy and Bubbe were willing to spring for Kosher pizza (Fresh not frozen) for lunch. That was enough for Michael, who then was all in, and even brought his bicycle. He was up to a 20-inch tire model now. Mike was always in a hurry to get everywhere, and waiting was not his favorite hobby. That was mathematics and that guy sure loved his numbers, how they fit together, and how numbers worked. Still in an effort to develop more patience and discipline, his parents had recently signed Michael up for Judo. The sight of an 8-year-old in a white Judo uniform, confident and disciplined, was pretty nifty. Steve loved to watch him at practice, but getting him to lessons, like most kid management details fell by default on his mother, Rita.

The girls were another story. Exercise was not their "thing". Both said it was "nebby" which was slang for nerdy. Yael, the oldest, set the tenor for the other two girls. Having the eminent good sense to be born first, like a member of a Royal family, Yael felt free to make decisions and issue decrees: "They were too grownup to ride bikes and besides, there wasn't room for the bikes anyways in the van." Yael was chock full of self-proclaimed "awesomeness." Still, she could be a thoughtful soul, when she wanted to be, which was most of the time. Yael brought some homemade biscotti that she had baked for everyone. They were sure to be "awesome".

Shira, was often under the shadow of her older sister, Yael. Steve often wondered if she should unionize. Older than Michael, but younger than Yael, Shira had recently come into her own with the self-awareness of her abilities in art and music. The recognition gave her confidence and pleasure. She could, and often did, spend hours drawing pictures and playing the piano. The above assumed, that Shira was not busy playing with her best friend Rachel. It was great for her parents to see her blossom.

Following close behind when they started on the path, was Raisa who was the leader of the tribe, i.e. the oldest child in her family. Raisa was very smart and knew it. At only age eight, and she already knew all of the Greek Gods. Why this was important, Steve did not know, but it was to Raisa. She attended the same private school where her mother Jan taught. Raisa was like a wise eight-year-old teaching instructor to her four-year-old twin sisters, who today were not along for the adventure.

Raisa was close to both Yael and Shira. It was Steve and Ann's frequent effort, that the cousins spend more time together. But like many things in life, such things were not within the control of even the best-intentioned grandparents. In any case, that would be ultimately up to the someday, grown up cousins, themselves.

They continued on the walk, with Rita playing point in an effort to see how far ahead Michael had gotten on his bike. Ann picked up the rear, holding the hand of the youngest Kayla, age five. Ann loved holding her hand and wondered how much longer Kayla would let her do that. Kayla was now her own person and had definite likes and dislikes now. Crunch, crunch, crunch, Ann thought the frozen leaves sounded like someone eating Grape Nuts breakfast cereal. Kayla loved stomping on the leaves and frozen puddles in her red shiny rain boots. This slowed Kayla and Ann down, but she didn't mind. Ann was in Bubbe Heaven, surrounded by her little angels. Lately, The Angels had not been getting along especially, Yael and Michael. It was constant guerilla warfare between the two. It was also a pain, Ann thought. Hopefully, the proffered bribe of pizza would keep their behaviors in reasonable check.

Ann let her mind wander. Forest Trails were good for that. Wandering. Pondering. She wondered what the grandkids would be like when they grew up and whether she and Steve would be around in good enough shape to really know them. She hoped so. She prayed that they would be happy, no matter what they did. Hoped they would meet someone and have children. Ann felt pretty fortunate that her children had.

Just then Ann heard trouble ahead, the whole forest could:

"You tried to put a stick through my bicycle spokes!" Yelled Michael. He spoke with the injustice that came from having an older sister who knew how to push a younger brother's buttons.

"I did not." Said the doe eyed Yael. "I was just going to draw a picture in the sand when you came flying in." Possible, not probable. Yael had a slight curve to her smile. Guilty as charged thought Ann.

Yael and Michael were always fighting. It was beyond annoy-ing, it was exhausting. Family rooms, bathrooms, dinner table, restaurants, no place was safe from a sudden outbreak of war between the two antagonists. Yael usually was the catalyst. But not always. Michael hadn't learned yet how to blow it off and ignore his sister's mischievous efforts.

Instead, Michael jumped off his bike, adopted a martial art attack pose, and uttered what he thought was a blood curdling yell:

"Hi, Yaaaaaa."

It was pretty impressive for a 7-year-old brother. It was loud enough to turn milk into cottage cheese. Yael's eyes widened. Maybe trying to put the stick in his spokes was not such a good idea.

Steve and their granddaughter Shira were ahead, still talking, not paying attention to the skirmish. Figured, Ann thought. She was going to have to handle the dispute, herself.

But the war widened to include a new contestant, Raisa:

"Hey, you can't pick on my cousin like that. Knock it off." Raisa was very protective of her two favorite female cousins. Though small, she was feisty. She put up her fists like a boxer. Raisa, in short, was a pistol. She was straight, true and always let you know that she knew what was best. She usually was, especially, if someone was hassling her younger sisters or cousins.

Ann sighed and thought for a moment. She had to settle this dispute now before Shira was dragged into the mess. She let go of Kayla's hand and made the universal Bubbe timeout sign by forming a "T" with her two hands:

"Timeout. We've had enough." A firm voice was important. Ann decided to resort to the grandparent's popular Threat vs. Bribe technique:

"Raise your hand if you're still interested in going out for pizza." 4 hands immediately shot up, Kayla's a few seconds later. Ann checked her watch. They had only gone .5 mile so far, pathetic. At this rate, they would never make 1 mile, let alone 2 miles:

"Right now, I don't think you are gonna earn any pizza at your current rate and behaviors. How about I up the ante to include a frozen dessert drink if you all do 2 miles by 1130?" This was a serious, expensive upgrade especially with kosher food.

Yael set off at a brisk pace with the rest following. Even Kayla tried to keep up.

It wasn't easy. But then, why it should it be? About 1 hour later, they gave up. Kayla did her best. As the youngest and smallest, it was hard for her 18-inch legs to keep up with her older siblings. But she would eventually catch up. Of this future fact, Ann and Steve had no doubt. Like many grandparents, their DNA had been engineered to eliminate any doubt factor, when it came to their grandchildren. Ann looked at her step counter and called it a win. They had gone 1.57 miles in 2 ¾ hours. They had missed both goals of 2 miles by 1130 am. But not by much. They all went off to the best kosher pizza and dessert drinks Chicago could offer.

That wasn't saying much, especially to Steve. Paying $30 for a single plain old cheese pizza was highway robbery in Steve's mind. But it was Kosher and had the certification on the wall to prove it.

The Ba Tempe (Hebrew for Tasty) Original Pizza Emporium was located in West Rogers Park where the Orthodox lived and prayed. It was well known for their whole wheat kosher pizza and their amazing frozen desserts including their famous Frozen

Chosen. (Chocolate ice cream, mixed with chocolate chips with whipped cream on top.) Their "village" had about 5,000 inhabitants in the immediate neighborhood. Besides the Shuls and schools, it had its own kosher bakery, grocery store and gift shop. It was a self-contained Kosher Island in the big city.

On the way back, walking to their house, Steve found himself talking with Yael. Yael was a smart girl, really, a teenager now. She asked Steve and Ann many questions on everything. Yael was a thoughtful thinker when she wasn't busy tormenting her brother. That alone seemed to be a full-time job.

"So where do we go when we die?" No introductions here. Teenagers blurt out whatever they are thinking, kind of like a brain burp. Steve thought for a minute. Then said: "That's a very good question." Teenagers needed reassurance that their burped thoughts were always appropriate. Steve thought some more. Wished that Ann had taken this question. No question, Ann was far more spiritual. Steve decided to give it a go: "To be honest

(What else was he going to be?), I'm not sure. It's the big question that everyone has to deal with." Well, duh.

Like many teenagers, Yael was impatient, she wanted an answer right away. So far, her grandfather had just given her a serving of intellectual mush. Steve realized he served what was really a nothing burger. He decided to try again: "I know our faith believes we are all brought back to life when the Messiah returns. (Steve was careful on this religious stuff with the kids, which they frankly knew better.) Your Bubbe believes we live on in the hearts of our loved ones."

"I already know that. I talked to Bubbe first." Really? Steve is pouring his gut out only to find he is only a second choice for the existential questions of life? Well, Steve could be deep too, when the occasion or teenager called for it:

"My friend Neil says this life/death thing is part of the deal. You can only be born if you die at the end. He says think about your kids…we gotta exit to make room for the new crew." Neil was a venture capitalist in a good way-How does the deal benefit the most people, including himself. Kind of comforting in a strange, capitalistic way. Steve still hadn't answered her question, but he moved in for the kill, anyways:

"While I'm not sure, I figure the soul has to go somewhere when we die. Spirit energy doesn't dissipate. The energy, like a radio beam going off into space, keeps on moving and is bouncing off the stars for its next adventure. Something or someone created this universe, and it all must fit together, somehow. At least, I hope so. Anyways, we, and especially you, have a lot of time before you need to think about it."

"Huh." Was all she said, and she ran ahead to their house to join the other kids. So that's all there was to it. That was another thing about teenager-short attention spans, even for Life's biggest questions. Steve tripped on the sidewalk, which was heaving, then caught himself. Such was life. Trip and fall. Lo que sera, sera. (Whatever will be, will be.)

21. The Dream Team.

That night Steve fell asleep quickly, deeply. Thoroughly. How could he sleep so well wasn't something Steve was always able to do, sometimes, it took a while for his mind to disengage before he fell asleep. It was also tough to re-engage when he woke up. Like today, for instance. He tried starting on his morning routine and thought about taking a nap. He drifted off a bit then opened his eyes to find himself in a bright orange kayak with Ann. She looked happy. Steve was not so sure how he felt. There they were, in a middle of a deep blue lake surrounded by pine trees. Was it Minnesota? How did they get there? Was Steve napping? Must be a dream, had to be. But he wasn't sure, and how did they end up in a bright orange kayak? Ann had talked about buying him one for his birthday, but Steve demurred, saying he could think of drier ways to get hurt. Anyways, unless it was one of those lighter, folding origami kayaks, the schlepping factor would be a 10+ on a factor of 10. Must be a dream, thought Steve's consciousness, and that was ok. Relaxed that he had hopefully figured out it was a dream, Steve breathed out and looked up. The sky was a deep black and had twinkling stars that looked like white LED lights. Steve felt that he and Ann were in one of those immersive Van Gogh tourist attraction extravaganzas that were still touring the country, Starry Night. Huh, that was a funny thing about dreams- they seemed so rich, so vivid in glorious colors, sometimes they seemed more colorful than real life.

"You ok there, slugger? You must have nodded off." Said Ann. She seemed more than ok with this dream, but then again it wasn't her dream. Or was it? Fair point. Ann and Steve talked about their dreams often. He wasn't sure what other couples did. For the most part, people didn't share what movies played in their heads at night. Ann had dreams where people were chasing her, or she was falling. When these dreams, nightmares really, woke Steve up, he would try to wake Ann up before she screamed further or worse yet, fell out of bed. But that's what couples did, they shared the good and the bad. When Steve would be groggy after Ann had a tough night, he would wish they could share a little less, so he could sleep a little more.

"Doing good." Steve looked and thought he saw a landing far off into the distance. Since this was a dream, he thought he should be able to bring the canoe landing closer through his mind. He couldn't -guess, it wasn't that kind of dream. "Ok, if we paddle now to Joel's Landing? (Steve had never met Joel but figured he had to be a good guy, for having a landing named after him.) All this water makes me wanna pee." Waking up to pee every night was now a regular practice for many middle-aged men, almost a hobby for Steve. Well, the hobby beat the embarrassing alternative.

They both started paddling. Because this was a dream, his left shoulder didn't ache at all. Steve had snapped two tendons in his left shoulder on Valentine's Day several years before. Yes, this was the same shoulder that he injured again after the disagreement with a car. The earlier time, he had been doing yard work trying to score points with his wife. Steve had tripped on a root, was knocked unconscious, and found his left arm was on strike when he came to. His shoulder hadn't been the same since, even with surgery. His old friend Brad was right, yard work can be the work of the devil and should be avoided at all physical cost.

He and Ann were working well as a paddling team on the water, dip and pull, dip and pull. Sometimes he let Ann do most of the work but then again, he carried the kayak to the water and assembled it. At least, that's what he assumed. The nice thing about dreams, was that a person could start at the good parts and skip the drudgery of everyday life. Well, at least he did in this dream.

When they were about 500 yards from the dock, a tall, muscular man in his mid-twenties pulled alongside in an alumacraft canoe. It was funny, he and Ann had one just like it, that was a bear to lift and move onto their car. After his surgery, they made the logical decision to replace it with the kayak which weighed less than half as much and fit easily in the back trunk when it wasn't assembled.

"Hey, Poppy, it's me, Dennis, wanna grab brunch at the diner?" Well, that was a no brainer. What grandparent didn't want to spend time with their grandson? But wait, how did he know that? But Ann seemed to recognize him, too in the dream:

"How's the ecology project going?" Dennis, a handsome Nordic type with blond hair was getting his PHD in ecology at the University of Minnesota. He was studying the mating habits of Loons, which predate Ducks by millions of years. Recently, the number of Loons had a precipitous decline. Why scientists weren't sure, so Dennis made it his mission to find out the reasons why. He liked nothing more than being in the field.

Dennis jumped out and helped to tie their boat along the dock. The three of them walked up to the restaurant -Cozy's. Cozy's was a tired breakfast joint in Two Harbors, some 30 odd miles North from Duluth on old Hwy 61. Dennis's cousin Michael had bought it on a whim, and it was managed by Michael's older sister Yael who was a professional baker. It was the only Kosher breakfast joint/bakery for over 100 miles. As a younger brother, Michael took real pleasure in now being his older sister's boss. Besides, Michael didn't know what to do with all his money, anyways. Assisted by his father, a CPA, Mike had invented an accounting program that was based on artificial intelligence and stored in the Cloud. Steve and Ann were not exactly sure how it worked but it did and was quite successful. Beyond successful.

One of the twins taking their order, had just received a post card from their sister, Raisa, the CIA agent. Really, their older sister was a spy.

"Hi Poppy and Bubbe, back already?" It was their granddaughter, Heather. With her blond hair and blue eyes, at 5 feet-10 inches, she looked like a beautiful Viking Warrior Princess- which she was. Heather was here working during summer vacation while she applied to veterinary school.

Her fraternal twin sister, Holly, was assisting behind the bakery counter. They were so close and yet so different. Each was their own person. Holly was spending her summer perfecting her rock-climbing skills and trying to figure out her next occupational move. She had time. No need to rush. Maybe she should become a spy like their sister Raisa. Really. A real spy.

Raisa had always been a quick learner, especially in foreign languages, and she had been encouraged to apply to the CIA by her Poppy. The two of them spent countless hours on pretend spy missions and training in Indian Boundary Park when Raisa was in grade school. Now Raisa was stationed in Vienna, Austria. Sometimes goofing off, does pay off- like her Poppy always said.

It was shaping up to be a remarkable summer. Almost all of the cousins were working and living together in Michael's large cabin in Two Harbors. With the fishing, hiking, rock climbing, camping and family meals, it was going to be the summer none of them would forget. Thankfully, they all knew it.

Granddaughter Kayla was working the cash register in a misguided effort that this would help her math, but she had not inherited the math gene from her father. She didn't care anyways for she was going to be a social worker like her mother.

The only cousin who was missing, besides Raisa, for the summer extravaganza was Shira, who was busy at a summer long music fellowship at the University in Minneapolis. She said that music was the best way to express feelings and that she did quite well. Shira hoped to debut her first Symphony that Fall. She was busy but happy. Shira came up as often as she could.

Like Ann often said, she and Steve were rich in grandchildren.

Time to order. Steve didn't care if he was in a dream or not, he was still hungry:

"I'll have the vegaroni omelet with spicy cheese, and with a double expresso exploding coffee, please." Maybe that would wake him up. Dream or no dream. The Vegaroni was a kosher substitute for sausage. "And for you, madam?" Wasn't that fancy? Ann went for the blueberry smoothie with a side of dry whole wheat toast. She liked to save her calories for lunch and of course, dessert.

It was a great meal. The omelet was superb, and the coffee was so strong it could be used in a post-surgical recovery room to revive unconscious patients.

Though he had nowhere he had to be, Steve started getting antsy. He had always been that way- always chafing to move forward. Before leaving though, he wanted to pay the restaurant check. No freebies for them. He was a little worried about how much this "adventure" was costing his grandson each month. "Don't worry." said Michael. "My tax advisor tells

me, sometimes you have to lose money to make money."
Steve wasn't exactly sure what he meant by that, but then
Steve lived on four zeros less of income than his grandson
each year.

Before leaving, Ann got most of the cousins to commit to a family bonfire at the burn pit at 9 pm, after the restaurant closed.

Steve didn't know why he was in such a hurry today, just was-
as usual. Ann was always encouraging him to slow down and if
not smell the roses, at least acknowledge the flowers' presence.
But there were so many things he wanted to get done -needed
to get done while he had the time. Steve acknowledged that cutting down on stress would be a good thing. He was pretty sure
the double expresso didn't help. Sure was good though.

Back at the dock, Dennis was there to assist. Steve wasn't surprised now to see him. That's what family members do for each
other. It's kind of like a personal free Triple AAA membership,
i.e., Almost Always Available to help. Then again, there are no
coincidences in dreams, anyways.

Ann and Steve were back in the kayak. Lake Superior was calm
that day. The couple never went on the Big Lake unless they
and the Lake were in a good mood. Lake Superior was just too
dangerous, if it wasn't perfect weather. Because the Lake was
essentially an inland ocean, it had an independent spirit and
could change its mood in a minute, they always paddled close
to shore. In spite of these precautions, Steve had once broken
an ankle from trying to step out of the canoe near some rocks in
Silver Bay.

They paddled on. The Lake was endless, amorphous. The grey
sky and Big Lake merged at the horizon, like a subtle George
Morrison painting. (Native painter who had lived in Grand Por-
tage. Mn. His work often dealt with the horizon.) Simply magnificent. The Native Americans called it Kitchi-gummi or great lake.
As it was that today. It was a clear deep blue that day. They paddled back to their resort just in time for a late lunch of pea soup
and salad. Then sleepy from all the exercise and morning carbs,
they decided to take a nap before the big campfire scheduled for
later. Steve, in particular, was in a time of life where naps were
no longer optional but required maintenance. Gotta recharge

those batteries before they get too far rundown. He laid down, wondering if one could nap during a dream? He was curious to find out but drifted off. He woke up groggy, several hours later, still unsure about the whole dream vs nap vs awake debate. Not that it mattered, anyways.

Steve grabbed his computer laptop and thought since he already had a headache, he may as while get back to work on his novel: Ben Retooled. It was about that slow drift to retirement and how his friends Larry and Brad had navigated it. Or not. He had close to 20,000 words done, about half a short novel, but felt like he had written himself into a corner that neither he nor his characters could get out of. How he had done that, he wasn't sure. Writing was hard, solitary work. Steve usually got up early, 4 or 4:30 am, and wrote for a few hours. Like exercise, a writer had to work on his craft, most days. Kind of like lifting intellectual weights- you didn't want the weights to be too heavy or too light. It wasn't easy, creating a believable, sometimes alternative world where your characters lived. Steve felt that when he was writing a novel, the characters also lived in his mind. Ignore them like teenagers at your peril. Though he tried to restart the novel almost every day, the truth was he didn't have enough gas in the word tank to complete it. Steve figured he spent at least 2000 to 3000 hours plotting, writing and rewriting one of his books. Steve was already still trying to walk a couple hours a day and he had those pesky arbitrations awards to write. So, there he was. 800 to 1000 hours into Ben Retooled, and nothing to show for it except 18,493 words. He gave up and started reading a John Le Carre novel. Probably had read it before but usually wouldn't realize that until page 150. These Le Carre characters already felt familiar. Steve hoped his own characters would cut him some slack and give him some more time to finish writing his novel, but he doubted it.

At 6pm, Ann and Steve decided to walk to the next resort: The Lazy Fish, for dinner. In spite of their name, their restaurant was best known for steak. Steve got tired of the frozen fish that was passed off as fresh Walleye at many restaurants, so he was appreciative of the efforts the Lazy Fish made with a steak. And who could screw up a baked potato? So Steve was all in when Ann suggested the nice walk and dinner. It would leave them plenty of time to prepare for the campfire. They hopped on the

Lake Superior Hiking Trail and walked to their destination. Lake Superior was a little more restive and a little less blue. The waters still looked like a minty mouthwash. It was a glorious walk-in spite of the occasional, teenaged 75-year-old senior who would whiz by on their electric bike. Sometimes, their smiles were so broad that Steve almost believed the bike was deriving its power from the seniors' teeth. Then again, all that energy might be all connected. Huh, worth thinking or napping about.

Steve was going to grab for Ann's hand when she beat him to it. Then she looked at him quizzically, like a female Sherlock Holmes:

"Still glad I talked you into getting a cabin for the month while the grandchildren were up here?"

"Yeah, but we still have our own big blue lake in Chicago. Don't know why, I wasn't so eager to do it."

Ann knew Steve was just getting pretty settled in with his Chicago coffee club but didn't say anything. It had been more of a struggle for Steve to readjust to their new city, but guys were like that. Tough to regain their sense of direction after a lifetime of work. Unlike many guys who seem to flounder, Steve would figure it out. He better. Between the kids, the book clubs and exercise classes, Ann had more than enough to keep busy than dealing with a bored, lonely husband.

"Well, you did. The cousins won't get many opportunities to get together like this before life scatters them." Ann was still amazed that their Michael was able to convince his cousins to come up for the entire summer. He even made an excel spreadsheet for each participant that listed the advantages and disadvantages for spending the summer together. Surprisingly, they almost all agreed. Then again, Michael was a natural born salesperson. As smart as Michael was, his EQ (Emotional Quotient) was even higher than his IQ. (Intelligence Quotient). He already had the big lake house and Yael had already committed to the bakery for the summer while she waited to see if she had been accepted to the CIA (Culinary Institute of America). The stragglers were few and far away: Raisa was busy keeping the world safe in Austria, while Bela in Minneapolis, promised, absolutely swore, to come up any time her music gave her a break.

Before they knew it, Ann and Steve reached the Lazy Fish. His stomach grumbled his agreement. It was time for a leisurely dinner. Steve's stomach ordered a medium well-done ribeye with a baked potato, no sour cream, as he was pretending to be health conscious. Ann went for the Berry Chicken Salad made with wild blueberries.

By the time they started walking back, the sun was beginning to set. Funny, the sunset looked the same as the sunrise, which made sense to Steve, because it was the same light coming from the same Sun. Ann, however, believed that there was a subtle difference and thought the soothing sunset with its blue and reds, was more orderly than what she considered the more chaotic, angry sunrise. As Ann was the painter, Steve was inclined to believe that Ann would know better. She usually did. Steve was just happy that he brought his flashlight, and he was with his girl. Dusk and darkness came quickly on the Northshore.

They made their way back to the burn pit. It was located behind Michael's cabin and not far from his restaurant. Someone had already started the fire in the pit that was a large 30-foot circle that had some old half pine tree benches. Because of the tall 50 feet Pines that surrounded the old A frame cabin, people couldn't see Lake Superior but could sure hear the waves crash in. Hopefully, no one could see the fire either, which was no longer permitted under law. The crackling of the fire almost sounded like popcorn popping and the smoke seemed to follow the gathered crowd no matter where they sat. Most of the cousins were already there and Dennis was playing a guitar- some acoustic version of a Crosby, Stills and Nash tune. Steve remembered the song but couldn't quite place it. Then again, it had been decades since Crosby and all were a thing. Still, it was magical. Ann sat off by herself when suddenly Shira showed up, complete with her Cello. Steve had certainly not been expecting Shira, but he had a sneaking suspicion that Ann knew and that's why she was sitting off to the side. Shira and Ann had always been close. When Shira went through her terrible two's phase, only Ann could calm her down from her tantrums, which were epic. Somehow Ann had always been able to reach Shira and first reached her by giving her an old blue electric blanket. While it didn't keep Shira warm, it did act as a weighted therapy blanket. The theory behind the blankets was the weight, made the subject feel more secure, almost like getting a continuous hug. Shira slept with it every night until her late teens when the blanket was so frayed, and the wires were so exposed, that Shira looked like a suicide bomber. But the old security blanket worked, and Steve wouldn't be surprised to find that Shira had it packed away safely for emergencies like now. Shira was not only working on her master's thesis in music, she was trying to decide whether to continue her music studies or go to medical school. Ann had faced a similar dilemma when she was trying to choose between becoming a professional painter in Paris or marry Steve and join the practical, read non-artistic, real life, where people had homes, families and a normal life, whatever that was. Steve hoped Ann hadn't regretted her choice. At least, not too much. We all have to make choices. And most of them don't give do overs.

Steve thought for a minute about walking over and joining the conversation but decided not to, even before Ann held up her universal wait ten-minute Index finger.

Steve was right, in waiting to walk over, the two were engaged in a heavy discussion. Ann was being earnest, almost painfully so: "What you have is a good problem- being admitted to both the University of Minnesota Music PHD Program and University Medical School are both great choices. You have options, something, many people don't get."

But Shira was having none of it: "I don't know what to do-what if I make the wrong decision?"

Ann chuckled: "There is no wrong decision, what does your heart tell you?"

Shira whined: "Just tell me what to do. That's why I drove up here- You always know what to do."

Ann had had enough: "That's a load of baloney. Worse yet, that's a cop out."

"Mom told me about the painting fellowship that you turned down at age 23. How did you know what to do?"

Ann decided to level with her: "I didn't. I just made the best educated guess I could." Ann looked at Steve: "I lucked out, pretty well."

Ann smiled but Shira pouted: "That doesn't help." Ann now called Steve with the same index finger, she had enough of this pity parade: "It's not supposed to- you'll figure it out or you won't. I'm betting you will, the first time. If you don't, you'll try something else. We have faith in you." She gave Shira a hug.

Shira felt a little better, not as good as holding her blanky, but pretty close. Just then Raisa walked in. This was unexpected, even in a dream.

This was great news. Raisa would know what to do, always did, always would. That kind of innate confidence was common among first-born children and in Raisa's case was well de-served. She was smart, confident and always willing to speak her mind.

Shira was the first to speak: "So good to see you! I was so sur-prised when you texted you were coming."

Raisa was beaming: "I had some vacation leave to burn before the end of the month and miss this shindig? No way, no how. I'm just glad you could put down your musical notes for a bit and come up here. Good to see you, too."

Shira and Raisa had always been close, from the time they were little children. Even though their sibling parents weren't, like Ann said: You can't force closeness. Quite the opposite for their children. Shira and Raisa talked or texted at least once a week. They walked quickly into the house to plot and catch up.

At the fire, Yael was helping the twins make their smores using imported Kosher Belgian chocolate. Standing behind Yael, enjoying it all, was Michael. The summer was turning out even better than he could have ever imagined. And imagination is what led to his A.I. invention in the first place.

The fire was burning brightly now. Dennis was managing it. The fire crackled every now and then as if it was chuckling with everyone. Maybe it was. The fire smoke gave off a natural smokey odor that smelled crisp. Not to be forgotten, Lake Superior sent a cooling mist that came over and made the cool night even colder. Still, the laughter and affection kept everyone warm.

Steve looked up at the stars. They seemed closer, brighter here outside of the big city. Steve thought of one of his favorite paint-ings: Starry Night by Van Gogh. Next, he picked out the Big and Little Dipper. He wondered what all the stars meant and how the ancient ones stared at the same stars and planets. What did they think about? What did they care? Deep thoughts, huh.

Steve found himself holding hands with Ann and gazing at his progeny. He felt pretty happy. Steve turned to talk to Ann and then THUMP! Steve found himself on the floor of their bedroom in Chicago. His right side hurt like the dickens. He must have fallen suddenly and woken up in pain from his dream. Or did he? Right now, achy and tired, he really didn't care. He gingerly climbed up the covers back into bed. Reached over for Ann and when he found her, he went back to sleep.

22. Steve and Ann for the Ages.

Even after the vaccines, life had not returned to normal. Or maybe, it was a new normal. Even with vaccine boosters, people still developed Covid. Age, weight, exercise, preexisting conditions, vaccine status all played a role in how serious a person's response to yet another round of Covid was. There were still holdouts to the vaccine, and they fared far worse in both hospitalizations and death. Then there were those who still limited their interactions outside their homes and still did not go to indoor restaurants, movie theaters and the like due to an abundance of caution. Ann and Steve's families were prudent but like most who had gotten the vaccines and boosters, they were no longer wearing masks in public. They remained vigilant and flexible to the virus. Their children, also vaccinated, continued to grow happy and strong.

Ann and Steve, being older and more vulnerable, were a little more careful, and would don a mask at crowded indoor events like movies. While they would still meet friends, they tried to meet outdoors or get takeout. But in spite of their efforts, they still came down with Covid several times.

Most times, their symptoms were mild, but Ann did have one major response and ended up in the hospital even after taking the wonder drug Paxlovid. Ann's first sign that something was wrong was when she lost her sense of smell and taste. This was a common early symptom of Covid. For a serious cook like Ann, that alone was a serious loss. From there, it was scary how quickly Ann's health deteriorated over just a few days. It was touch and go for a while for Ann and she ended up on oxygen in the hospital. Steve still shuddered at the memory of seeing his Ann look so frail under the breathing mask and he, not being able to do anything except hold her hand for hours at the hospital. But she recovered and most of her strength returned over time. Others were not so lucky.

People still died from Covid, and others continued to have serious lingering effects months after coming down with it. Sam the Contractor, after first thinking he had recovered, developed Long Covid in which some of his symptoms returned with a vengeance. Sam still felt fatigued even months later, and retained a persistent, painful cough. It reached a point where Sam had to weigh an unplanned early retirement versus going on disability. Problem was Sam wasn't ready for either. Even more frustrating to Sam was how people responded to him after he would explain he still suffered from Long Covid: "When are you going to feel better?" or worse yet "Have you thought about seeing a psychologist?" Well-meaning but ill- advised friends would ask unanswerable, read stupid questions. Sam ground his teeth so much, trying to hold his temper, that Sam thought he was going to have to see a dentist.

To both Ann and Steve, Ann's illness and hospitalization served as a reminder how fleeting life was and how they couldn't take anything or anyone for granted. So, the couple didn't and found themselves spending the summer up at Two Harbors with the kids. They even loosened up their spending, figuring they would rather die with lots of memories rather than leaving lots of money. Funny thing was, they were still putting off revising their wills and making funeral plans, almost as if failing to do so, would keep them alive longer. Sure, they would talk about it, a bit, but when push came to shove, they would rather sit. As long as they were together. Somehow, some way, some place- they believed they always would be.

23. You can always find it at Cera's.

Ann did most of the shopping without complaint. She also did a lot of household chores that way. It wasn't fair. Steve was oblivious, or pretended to be, of how much work went into keeping their household going. Occasionally back in the day when he was working, he would claim he didn't help more because he was working full-time but the truth was Ann worked as many hours as he did. It took Steve a long time, to lessen the genetic male blinders he wore, that kept him from noticing and volunteering to help with all the chores. Now, sometimes Ann didn't even need to ask.

Well, today Steve was going to go shopping. He didn't need no stinking list! Anne reminded him to get celery, radishes and 5 pounds of carrots. He hadn't gotten any exercise yet that day, so he decided to take his bike. The key to their continued mobility was fitting in some exercise into their daily routine. Exercise wasn't something a person could simply hire out. Besides, by biking, he wouldn't be looking for a parking space for his car when he got back. He grabbed a backpack and was off. Steve had decided to go to Cera's on Ridge. They had great produce that included some interesting ethnic varieties he had never tried. Maybe he should. Steve was on a recently acquired, life-long mission of finding new veggies that didn't bore him. He was thinking of trying a new diet that he called the Hershey Plan: just coffee and chocolate til dinner every day. Since it wasn't Friday, maybe he could even see Russ, the store manager. Even though Russ worked a lot, and Steve went to Cera's a lot, their schedules hadn't meshed, and it had been several months since he had seen him. But that's how it often is with guys, while they need to tend to their friendships, they don't always do that and the bonds weaken. Women know better- perhaps that's why they make better gardeners, they know how to tend.

Steve made a beeline for Russ's office, but he wasn't there. Steve thought he might be working the grocery aisles, so Steve decided to do his shopping while he loitered. Though he didn't have a list, there was a strong probability that he could use some more whole grain Wasa Crackers. Steve had Wasa for breakfast every day. While some people including his wife compared its taste to packing material, after age 50, one could never have too much fiber.

Steve went searching for the crackers and mistakenly went to the cracker aisle. He should have known better, for the Cera's store layout no longer matched the aisle descriptor signs. Russ had changed the physical layout when Covid was at its height to keep workers busy. Rather than admit he was doing it to keep employees working, he claimed he did it to keep the employees from getting bored. Steve didn't know about that, but he did know it kept shoppers like himself in state of constant bewilderment. So, he wasn't surprised when he found no crackers in the cracker aisle, but he was pleasantly surprised to find a new and improved Beatrice, the retired cop, picking out some gourmet dog treats that promised to clean the dog's teeth and stimulate their gums. Beatrice looked new and improved because she had dropped 30 pounds since the last time he had seen her. She looked 10 years younger, too. When Steve asked her what her secret was, her answer was telling:

"There's no secret, I finally got rid of my 1000-yard -police stare. It took over a year and moving out of the city. My dog Frankie had a lot to do with it. Frankie is a happy little Frankfurter breed who keeps me smiling. We go out hiking on the flat trails every day." She laughed again.

Steve thought for a minute about what she said. People sometimes forgot how much continuous stress Chicago Police Officers were under on an hourly basis. That feeling of stress didn't disappear when Beatrice got off work and took off her bullet proof vest. It dissipated only when she left her job, moved out of the city and got an energetic happy dog.

"Glad you are doing better. You look great."

"I feel great. Finally getting enough exercise and it really helps me feel better. Much better. When are you going to leave the city?"

People who had moved out of the city felt it was only a matter of time before their family and friends would join them. But that wasn't always the case. There was no way, Steve and Ann, especially Ann, were going to leave the city, with their grandkids growing up there. It was a magnetic draw without the possibility of reverse polarity.

"Never, we're all in- for all time." Funny, how that works. Steve continued: "But don't be a stranger. The guys would love to see you at coffee, at least once in a while."

"How about we shoot for once in a blue moon? That sounds more realistic." Beatrice laughed. It looked good on her. "I got an art show at Bark, the artists bar in Garfield, coming up in 3 months. I'll have more free time after that." Steve had noticed that about some of their friends who found it difficult to make plans since Covid. "Never admit and never commit." One of them used to say. Or maybe it was the other way around. Steve still hoped to see Beatrice around the fishbowl of life, but he couldn't force a change in her direction: "Well, good luck with that, I'll let Theo know." Theo would care. He always did.

Steve finally found Russ in the frozen food aisle where one of the freezers sounded like it was going through an asthma attack. Russ and another worker were loading 2 grocery carts with frozen food. That was the thing about Russ- he was a rare boss who pitched in, wherever he could, when there was work to be done.

"You here for the Shiva? (Jewish Memorial Meeting for the dead.) This freezer is dying and on its last legs. Good to see you, it's been a while."

Russ was right, it had been too long. Steve wondered how his friend was doing:

"How is everybody doing in your family?" Since Covid, people didn't assume anything. They couldn't.

"Doing pretty well, I got no complaints." Well, Russ probably did but he wasn't one to complain, except about the mechanical equipment at the store. As the freezer proved, it didn't do any good, anyways.

24. Another Cup of Coffee.

Coffee Klutch patron members Tim and Stu were early. Or maybe it was a breakout group. Sometimes guys needed to talk about something without the whole world or least their part of the world listening in. From outside the grocery store it looked pretty intense, so Steve let them be and sat in his car for a bit. He could always fiddle with his phone.

Phones were pretty impressive. People never had to look up and talk anymore. People were not tethered to their phones but rather bound to them in an unhealthy way that made it hard to breathe. People always had to have their phone within arm's reach. Some people, Steve included, found it difficult to even go to the bathroom without their communication lifeline to relax. It was at the same time both annoying and a necessary distraction. An electronic emotional crutch.

After about 20 minutes, Steve got tired of waiting. He had things to do and places to go. But rather than get ahead of the day, he sauntered into Cera's, pretending he had just arrived. A lot of seniors did that- showing up late and pretending they were busy.

But the two men were still at it. Intensely. They were probably talking about Stu's son Gary, again. Usually were. Even though Tim was busy with his real estate business, he still found time for friends. He was good that way. Sad to say, not many people were that way anymore. People had time for their phones, 401ks, and Facebook but relationships? Not so much, anymore. Tim, Stu and the others recognized the true value of having what a therapist would call, a mutual support group- not that any self-respecting men's coffee klatch would ever call it that.

Steve was right, they were talking about Gary. Again.

Stu's son Gary was permanently adrift, and Stu couldn't figure how to get him back to shore. Stu loved him dearly, but sometimes it wasn't enough. Gary had run through a bunch of colleges, relationships and jobs, relying on his parents to financially bail him out. Usually, they did. But there comes a point where parents can't financially or emotionally carry them anymore, the burden was too much. Besides, where would their kids go when their parents were gone?

"Gotta let him go, stop paying for him let him sink or swim."

Easy for Tim to say that, his daughter Audrey was a brain surgeon. Ok, she was a gastroenterologist. She could make your gas pass, faster and better. Really. On the other hand, Tim had invested wisely and often on his smartest child: Private schools, tutors, etc. Money didn't always push a child across the finish line, but it didn't hurt. Usually. If money was a tool, rich people and their progeny always had a bigger tool box.

"Gary is working, again. He's a waiter at that fancy new restaurant called Burp." Maybe their kids could refer customers to each other.

"But is he paying his own way?" Being smart, Tim already knew the answer, but he waited semi-patiently, any ways.

"Mostly."

"What does that mean?" Steve really didn't understand for he didn't speak "Rich Folk".

Tim was quite fluent in "Rich Folk", having made his first million, at least on paper, before he was 30, he was confident and not afraid to share his opinions:

"Let me guess, he still has a corporate credit card for dining and whining." Gary was well known for his numerous complaints about his bad luck: in college, in relationships, in Vegas and in life. In general, Gary did not have the requisite amount of insight or accountability. Stu and his wife each blamed the other for Gary's short comings {Perhaps, they did care too much) but at the semi-ripe old age of 33, Gary had no one to blame but himself.

"Gotta cut him off." Tim was certain. Most parents were -of what other parents should do with their own children. Steve wasn't so sure about how to cut someone off the family support network including the family dole. He and Ann were lucky, their kids had always paid their own way. Mostly.

Steve decided to change the subject:

"So, how about the Bears vs. Vikings football game this Sunday? Anybody wanna watch it with me at Altman's? " Before law school, Steve didn't really care about football but watching the games at a bar brought his classmates together. Many were still his closest friends today. The groans and cheers watching a flat screen brought them closer than any discussion of feelings ever would. The game had grown on Steve. But Steve now had to pretend to be a Bears fan in Chicago if he had any hopes of finding someone to watch the game. Today no such luck:

"Nah, I got a brunch with the relatives." Probably, something his bride had set up.

"I got hockey practice with the mini mites. (Players under the age of 5. In Chicago, they taught males aggression early.) Hard to believe but at age 72, Tim was still coaching hockey. He was good that way. For that matter, so was Stu- as a volunteer for budding entrepreneurs on the South Side. Busy people still found time to help others.

Fred on the other hand, didn't have time or interest to waste on football: "Can't. I still am trying to find a spring that will fit your toaster oven. I've already had it over a week. Then, I have to get caught up in throwing out old Popular Mechanics Magazines. Toots (Fred's nickname for Beth) is threatening to throw out every issue older than 2015." Fred, once he undertook a mission, was unstoppable. It wasn't easy trying to manage an A.W.O.L., retired Naval Commander but Beth his wife, did her best. Fred knew he was lucky to end up with Miss Moose Lake of 1961. Very lucky.

Thus, it looked like Steve was going to be at the bar alone or be forced to watch it with the sound off at home. These were Ann's rules. It was fair but Steve didn't know what was worse- being stuck in a Bears Bar as a secret Vikings fan or no sound. No one to cheer with. Either case left a bad taste in his mouth even if he wasn't drinking ultra-low calorie beer. Steve glanced at his watch.

9 am. Fred stood up, didn't even need to look at his watch. Fred never did. He always knew what time it was. Time to go. Everyone shuffled off to feast on the remains of the day. They all felt better, knowing they had already accomplished something, even if they weren't sure what it was.

25. Party On!

The Fall Festival was long overdue. While people had gotten together every day to garden and had happy hour in the open gazebo, it just wasn't the same. Most people were still being careful. After all, Park Gables had held 46 consecutive Fall Festivals until Covid hit. So, shareholders were ecstatic, not just excited, when Rose and Sima, the Official Ladies of the Vine, announced on Facebook that Covid be Damned- the 47th Almost Consecutive Fall Festival. This year's theme: World Peas. Every year a different vegetable they grew was featured. This year was scheduled to be held the first Sunday of November and was going to be potluck where everyone brought a dish to share. It was still going to be held outside, provided the weather cooperated, for many people were still skittish over possible exposure to Covid. Yep, there it was, still hanging over their heads, but people were more than ready to keep moving forward with their lives. The Ladies of the Vine were, and they showed up to the party with their sundresses and sun hats. They even had their matching holiday sweaters, for the cool weather, courtesy of Kohl's. Thankfully, the weather had cooperated, i.e. in the low 50's, which was never a sure thing in the Windy City. Weather fronts blew in and out without any consistency, and Steve had yet to settle on a go to TV weather station.

They were all there, mostly except for the few that were still at higher Covid risk, or just plain unsocial. Then there were the losses. These losses all had names: Grace, Bob, Bill, Sue. Although, their building complex lost fewer people due to the Pandemic, there were still too many. They all had loved ones and their survivors were left to carry on somehow. But they now carried their dearly beloved ones too, and it was a stone laid upon their hearts. Heavy, ever present, ever painful. Steve didn't know how they did it-day after day. Steve was still half expecting to see their neighbors, Bob and Bill walk up to him and talk about the Chicago Cubs.

Still, the party was a great success. People had to double layer their Styrofoam plates to carry all their food. It was quite the selection. There was Barb's famous split pea soup and Annie's almost vegan potato salad. There were brats on the grill donated by the previous board of directors and the dessert table was completely covered. Rhubarb pie, brownies, apple cake, apple pie, homemade chocolate chunk cookies. Lemon meringue pie. It was quite the spread and calorie count. People had really out-done themselves and their stomachs.

But the real sugar high came from the long-delayed hugs and discussions that were welcomed and needed. People got caught up on each other's triumphs and reversals. Residents successfully compared records on marriages, births and deaths. It felt normal.

Then it was time for the awards ceremony. Each year the Garden Club handed out prizes that were hotly contested. But first those present had to endure the remarks of the M.C. Will DeYoung. Aged 76, Will was short and thick but still had a full head of grey hair. Some follicles have all the luck. A retired real estate attorney, who still favored Brooks Brothers suits even in retirement; today he was wearing a knit brown cardigan sweater. Will relished his few opportunities that he got to be a Master of Ceremonies and he had been practicing his material out in the garden. Steve felt it was cruel and unusual punishment to the plants. Will cleared his voice several times to get everyone's attention:

"Well, hello everyone, what a grand afternoon for a party! Wasn't the food and the company great? I want to thank all of the volunteers. My name is Will DeYoung, and I am your M.C. tonight. I am here to hand out the awards. It's a dirty job (get it?) but somebody's got to do it, so let's pro-seed and put our petal to the metal. Before we get started, can anyone tell me why the gardener didn't take the job? Because the celery wasn't big enough." There were several groans and only Will laughed.

Will got a little defensive but tried again any ways: "I am not a one trick peony!" This time there was no response from the crowd so Will continued: "The first prize is for flower of the year and the winner is very appropriately named: Rose!" Again, a slight response though Rose was excited and curtsied after she received the certificate.

Will sadly tried again: "I don't want to STEM your enthusiasm, but I know the next category helps put food on the table: best vegi-table. The winner is, gird yourself, is Brian!" Brian was shy and not one to tout his own horn but his gourds were amazing.

"That leaves one final award, for Gardner of the Year." Will paused for effect, like they taught him in Toastmasters Speech Club: "I want to read this one out loud for it is well deserved: In recognition of their years of faithful and devoted service, the Board of the Garden Club gives the 2022 Gardener of the Year to Katie and Earl." This time, everyone clapped loudly, for it was so well deserved. They had spent countless hours tending to the needs of the garden including weeding and getting others to start gardening. When they came forward to accept their award, Sima gave them a bouquet of roses. That was the end of the formal program, but people stayed until dark. It was a special night and a special place. The best part of the evening and there were many, was that they all knew it.

26. Final Cup of Coffee.

Steve got there later than Theo but that was par for the course. After all, Theo had been a serial entrepreneur and he was used to early hours. No one beat Theo to his appointments, no one. Heck, he was used to many hours, anyways. But what Steve wasn't used to was finding Theo laying his head on the table like a treasured Rib Roast:

"Theo, are you ok? What's wrong?"

"My vertigo has come back and its bad, kid, really bad."

"Sorry to hear that. Maybe you should go home and get some rest."

"I feel too dizzy to drive home. I gotta stick around. Ted wanted to drop off some peppers." Ted was a generous soul who didn't like getting up early. He had a weekend farm in Wisconsin. Ted liked to say that you could take a Country Irishman away from the farm, but you couldn't take the desire to farm away from a Country Irishman. Steve thought he understood what that meant.

205

The Rib Roast lifted his head slowly:

"But enough about me, how are you doing? You still taking the vinegar with your radioactive pumpkin seeds like I told you?" Only Theo could make Steve's prostate cancer treatment taste like an ill-advised smoothie. And he was still pushing the vinegar. It was enough to really piss Steve off. Literally.

"Enough of your half-baked home remedy cures." Though Steve appreciated Theo's concern. Mostly.

"It's not baked; the vinegar is boiled." Theo was a little defensive about how people criticized his home remedies that he got from the internet. It wasn't like he made it up. Steve thought some-where, somewhere- someone did.

"I'm getting by. Doctor says it's stabilized. I still got eye drops for the Glaucoma, too. Seem to be working."

"Don't forget your omega threes." Again, with the sardines. At one point, Theo suggested Steve lay the Sardines on his eyes prior to eating them. Yuck. Unbelievable. Still, Theo's concern was touching. It wasn't something guys put on display in groups, but they did have each other's back and could display that concern, if they wanted to, when they were one on one.

Steve preferred it sometimes when it was just he and Theo at coffee. He had learned a lot from the other guys, especially Fred and Tim. On occasion though, their suggestions were often over the top. Fred, for example, was a firm believer in always doing things his way or the offender risked being tossed in the sea. Then again, Fred had been a naval commander and was used to being in charge. Clearly, Fred was a fiercely independent man who liked to get his way. Steve still chuckled thinking over when Tim made the mistake of renting to Fred. Tim often told the story, of later when Tim installed a fake thermostat in Fred's office after Fred complained about the temperature, one too many times. Both Tim and Fred were impressive in their own way. They didn't make them like that anymore. Maybe they should.

Still, his other friend Theo had seen a lot and what was more, had lived a lot in his eighty odd years. Steve felt it was like getting a master class in street smarts from Theo without paying online tuition. And there was so much to learn, almost too much to absorb. So, Steve kept showing up to coffee day after day after his return from Sedona. Not to be morbid, but Steve wasn't sure how much longer this rodeo would be playing. Steve regretted not taking the time to talk to seniors like his grandparents and parents about their lives while they were still cogent and available. He wasn't going to make that mistake again. But he had repeatedly failed to so in the past, and there were no do overs for getting personal history. So, he went to coffee as often as he could and also shared as many family stories as possible to his children that they could reasonably tolerate. Like he told them: "There is no overdosing on family lore." But maybe there was. At least, they had inherited the family sigh, when he told them his Bar Mitzvah pranks for the umpteenth time.

Steve then thought about all the friends who were already on the other side of the grass as Theo liked to put it, who had already died. He was determined not to let Theo and the others be forgotten, at least in his mind. Maybe he would write a book about them some day. So, he decided to start that day by taking a mental photo of Theo for his long-term memory bank.

Theo was a vigorous man even in his 80's. He still had a full head of grey hair. His wife combed it every day. Theo shoveled his own snow and carried his own groceries. Theo even moved his own furniture when he shampooed his carpet. Steve was always volunteering to help but Theo would turn him down saying: He had arms, if he didn't use them, why have them? Fair point.

Theo did wear thick black glasses and was actually thinking about getting new hearing aids. They were cheaper now, after finally placed on over the counter. Theo wasn't cheap but he did like to shop around for a bargain. Exhibit A, the plaid flannel shirt, Theo bought that week at Costco. "Feel that quality." he urged. Just because he was older, didn't mean that he was a Chump, he would remind Steve. Of course, he still drove a car, his trusty 2011 blue Kia, and had even dragged a would-be carjacker 2 blocks on California Avenue. True story. Steve hoped he was half the man that Theo was when Steve reached his 80's. Theo looked forward to each and every day, viewing them as a gift to savor.

Just then Theo interrupted Steve's reverie:

"Hey guy, Wake up, wake up! For the last time, this ain't college where you can sleep through it! Class ended half an hour ago." (Theo hadn't been able to afford college. Times were different.)

But class wasn't over for just then, Ted and Rick had walked in. Rick's Jeep Renegade was not working, again. How did he manage to get to work each day? No wonder the pizzas he delivered were occasionally cold.

He was lucky that Ted was such a nice a guy and willing to drive 5 miles out of his way to pick Rick up. But that's what friends do and that's what these friends often did.

Rick offered to buy Ted an English muffin or an Irish scone to thank him.

To Ted, however, there wasn't a question as to which treat to take: "Well, as a self-respecting Irishman, I'm sure as hell, not gonna take an English muffin." Really? It had come to this? Edible patriotism?

In an effort to change the subject, Steve asked: "So what are you all doing for Thanksgiving?"

As a pizza procuring specialist, Rick knew that Thanksgiving was the busiest day for takeout pizza next to the Super Bowl. There were a lot of hungry people who end up alone on the couch during the big game. Might as well get stuffed crust pizza. Makes sense. At least your stomach isn't lonely. Steve hated Thanksgiving – it was a tough time for him thinking of past dinners with his parents. Not now, but long ago when he was single, done with law school, and trying to make it as a fulltime union atty on $13,000 a year. He knew he could get invited to someone's table, but he usually didn't want to explain his family's complicated history. At morning coffee in a different city, decades later, he never had to.

At morning coffee, Steve had a place where he still belonged. So did the others like Fred, Rick, Ted, Russ, Theo and the others who floated through. It wasn't home, but it sure was comfortable. Kind of like a well-used Lazy Boy that aged in sympathy with the people who sat on it. It just felt right. Most of the time, that was enough.

But Steve thought too, about the empty chairs and those people, who could no longer stop by and had been lost too soon. He stared at the empty chairs that should have been occupied. Friends like Parking Paul, Al, Ralph were gone and would not be walking in again. Others like Sam, who survived with Long Term Covid, now lived mostly in silent, painful anguish. Made no sense to Steve. It hurt, carrying that constant ache in his heart. He felt the pain at some point, most every day. Yet Steve figured those missing, wouldn't not want them hurting, but would rather have the remaining guys joking, laughing and just plain living. So that's what they did. Yep, that was pretty much all they could do.

27. Steve and Kayla.

It was a cold day in November. The sky was already getting ready for winter and had its steel grey hue. It is crisp outside and although the temperature reads 30, it feels like 20 to Steve when he scraped the morning frost off the car. Steve saw Crazy Larry on the side of the road at a bus stop. Dressed in a purple Vikings knit hat and long trench coat, Steve hopes he is warm enough. Sometimes, Steve would stop to pick Larry up and give him a ride. Hey, that's what friends do. But not always. Larry is talking to himself, and Steve has places to be, people to see so Steve pretends to himself that he doesn't see Larry until he is already past him. Friends do that too, pretending not to notice. Still, Steve is in a hurry because he had promised Kayla, his youngest granddaughter, that he would take her to the beach. Kayla loved the Leone beach where Touhy Avenue runs into Lake Michigan. It is a small beach located next to a smaller children's park. Apparently, the semi famous yet anonymous photographer, Vivian Maier hung out here for hours at end when she wasn't taking some of the thousands of street photographs she took unknown and unrecognized.

But Steve and Ann weren't unknown and unrecognized. They took pleasure in being Bubbe and Poppy to their grandchildren. Most of the time that was enough. Some people like Ron and Karen understood the grandparent gig right away, and their frequent Facebook postings detailed the ecstasy they felt when they were around their children. Others like Steve and Ann (Alright, mostly Steve) had to warm up in the important role. Some never understood it, and still others, never got the opportunity. But Steve got it now and that's why he was on his way at 10 am in the morning to pick up Kayla.

Kayla was already in her winter coat and was swinging her mittens from side to side. She was excited. The other kids were too old to be bothered with going to the beach and Steve was more than ok with that. Just the two of them, as usual.

"You ready to go down to the beach and the park with Poppy?"

"Oh yes, I got my pail for the rocks and seashells." Her brown eyes seemed to be smiling and Steve felt the warmth of her glow. There was nothing like Grandpa worship by his favorite 5-year-old.

"Did you go Potty yet?" Steve hated to be the potty police, but it was after Labor Day and all the park bathrooms were locked.

"Yes, poppy I did. Did you?" Kayla giggled. All the kids teased their grandfather about how often he had to stop to pee.

"Why, yes I did, thank you very much." Steve was still overly sensitive about the needs of his prostate even when discussing it with his major 5-year-old fan.

He grabbed her hand, and they were off to the car.

They drove down Touhy Avenue, past the cash checking office, and the 7-11 convenience store across the street. It did not pass Kayla's attention:

"Can, we have a Freeze Pop now, please?" Kayla must have thought including her Poppy in the request might make it more likely.

"No time now but maybe on the way home." Unlike parents, grandparents never paid the current dental price for spoiling their grandkid's teeth rotten. So of course, Steve took the kids out for snacks and then immediately dropped them off at their home before the sugars converted to energy surging, trouble-making carbohydrates. But like his good friend Ted advised when dealing with adult children, don't get mad get even, through the grandchildren. (Usually with sugar.)

Though he was happy to be out with Kayla, the current state of Touhy Avenue caused a significant sigh as always. One of the main east west arteries, Touhy Avenue was in the 30th year of a slow fade into oblivion. The crumbling infrastructure needs of the entire city were reflected on this tired street. There were numerous potholes, and many street corners were missing signs. The side-walks were even in worse shape. They had so much heaving and cracking, that it looked like the sidewalks were throwing up as if the concrete was saying, it couldn't take it anymore. Steve, again for the umpteenth time, silently cursed the long time Alderperson, but in truth he knew the troubles were far larger than one elected official. The problems of Chicago ran deep, and they seemed so numerous, that nobody knew where to start repairing them. "How about fixing some of the damn streets?" Steve mumbled.

"What was that, Poppy?"

"Nothing, sweet stuff." He had been reminded repeatedly by
his daughters not to swear in front of the kids. Swearing had
become such a problem, that the City had started a program
complete with yard signs that read Civil Chicago. Good idea but
waste of money. "Bet people would be less coarse if the streets
were better maintained." Drivers in Chicago had to tolerate
A LOT.

"Poppy, I'm not a sweet roll." Kayla giggled.

"OK, how about I call you honey bun?" Steve switched back to
grandpa mode. After all, that's why they had come back. Sweet
stuff was his nickname for Kayla the youngest. He had given her
that nickname because whenever he asked her what she wanted to do, she would say sweets and stuff.

"Honey buns are too sticky." She had a point. Kayla often did.
She was a smart girl. wise beyond her years. Beyond Steve's,
too. He enjoyed watching the grandkids grow like beautiful

flowers. Steve never knew, when and what they going to reveal. It was magnificent. It almost, but not quite, paid for their grandparents growing older and weaker. But as Neil said, that too, was part of the deal. "Once you're born, you don't come out of it alive." Fair enough. "A deal's a deal, even if you don't sign up for it. So, savor it, taste everything you can while you can." No question, Neil was a smart guy.

"OK, we'll stick with Sweet Stuff." Kayla and the other grandkids made him forget the faded streetscape. Memories of the long-gone Kosher shops and Shuls went back into his memory storage bins.

Soon, they were there. Their favorite park with some of the most desirable lakefront in Chicago. Not really maintained, as was usually the case in Chicago.

"Do you think we'll find any shells today?" Kayla asked as she grasped his hand walking down the path. Shells were her favorite thing to look for on the beach. The beach ran pretty far in either direction but was broken up by large boulders that had been placed there by man, in a futile attempt to protect the shore from further erosion by the hungry lake. The lake originally ran as far west as Western Avenue before man starting laying claim on the shore and filling it in. But ultimately, Lake Michigan was gonna do what Lake Michigan wanted to do. In this case, it meant reclaiming its lake front property and then some. Global warming meant that Lake Michigan could rise by 17 inches by the year 2030. People needed to plan accordingly. So far, they mostly hadn't.

Kayla took her plastic shovel and started digging. Scoop, slop. Scoop, slop. Kayla was a pretty efficient worker for a 5-year-old. Soon the water filled the hole. "Nothing here, Poppy." Like any self-respecting prospector, Kayla was eternally optimistic that her shells laid just beyond, in a hole that hadn't been dug yet. Steve on the other hand, limited his search for rock glass which was broken pieces of glass that had long ago been shaped and massaged by the water into smooth irregular rock shapes. He was particularly fond of green, almost translucent, pieces of broken 7 Up bottles. In this era of plastics, it was harder and harder to find. Maybe, today was the day. Steve was still a kid at heart.

Ann said that he was eternally AND terminally age 12. Whatever. Fine by him. Steve felt that exuberance made life more fun. It was rare that people could hold on to it. He thought of his friend Mike, gone 10 years, who was the most effervescent person he had ever met. He could light up a party room with just a smile and often did. Amazing. Mike was also thoughtful. Every day, he made tea for his wife and brought it upstairs to her. Taken by cancer, he still cheered people up until his final days. Steve knew he lived on in the hearts of his loved ones. Still, gone too soon. The good ones usually are.

Just then he heard a screech that he recognized as pure joy emanating from his granddaughter:

"I found it! Two of those." At age 5, grammar was just beginning. Who cared? At her age, Steve just wanted to encourage Kayla to do as much talking and thinking as she could.

Kayla ran up and shared her treasures that appeared to be 2 broken shells. She was ecstatic. And why wouldn't she be? True, they were not rare collectibles. But come on! What did it matter? The find made her eyes sparkle and Steve felt her radiant joy almost like a positive energy flow. Couldn't beat it.

"Tell you what, we'll put these in the treasure chest." Well, it really was a mostly empty 3-pound coffee can that had Kayla's name on it that they kept in their storage locker. It kept many of her treasures including other shells, several bird feathers and a polished red agate. Kayla had already learned the important lesson that what's treasured most, isn't always gold.

"Poppy, can we play in the playground?" It was small but lethal. In addition to the usual jungle gym and slide, it had several spinners that a person could sit upon and directing their weight, the spinner would spin indefinitely. Steve had ridden on it several times, gotten really dizzy, and was properly afraid of it. Kayla knew that. She loved her poppy dearly but still enjoyed watching him get dizzy.

"Poppy, let's race." She was clever, she knew that Steve still liked a challenge.

"I'd like to, but it makes me dizzy."

"Is poppy chick-en?" Kayla's siblings had done a fine job teaching their sister, the ways of the world, including how to over enunciate when they were teasing.

"Poppy isn't afraid." Steve didn't often refer to himself in third person. No need to.

They jumped on top of their playground spinners, and they were off to the races. Kayla spun quickly and was gleeful. For Steve, it was an altogether different experience, and the darn thing just would not stop. Even after going 10 times around. Maybe it was due to the oversized love handles he was carrying on his gut.. In any case, in frantic desperation, he called to Kayla for help: "You win, you win! Please help me stop." Steve felt that his body had become disconnected from his soul.

"Can we stop for a Kosher Slurpee when we go home?" Kayla had learned her negotiation skills from her brother who had taken a course in verbal Judo.

"Of course, just help stop me right now."

"Ok" she said now that the deal was established, and she hopped off. Holding out her hand, Steve reached for it but missed Kayla and flew around again. "Stop playing, Poppy, do you want to get off or not?" Steve felt nauseous but he could still hear his wife's voice in a pint-sized version.

"Yes, yes, just make it stop." Steve felt like he was extra in a horror movie where the evil clown would not stop the amusement ride.

"Well then, don't slouch and sit straight. You will stop, I promise."

And so, he did. Eventually, the evil ride slowed. Steve thought it should have a warning label.

But when he attempted to get off the so-called amusement ride, Steve found he couldn't stand straight, and he felt an awful case of vertigo coming on. Steve finally understood what Theo had been complaining about. He weakly sat down on the ground. It was filthy. All he could think about was that song from his youth: Dizzy by Tommy Roe.

Kayla was concerned: "Are you Ok, Poppy?" She sat down next to him. Steve's head seemed to stop spinning as much. Her concern was a salve on his dizzy soul.

"Poppy, mommy doesn't like it when we sit in schmutz (dirt). With that, she stood up, all 3 feet of her, pulled him up, grabbed his hand and pulled him to a bench nearby to sit.

The two of them sat quietly and stared at Lake Michigan. In and out. In and out. In and out. Kayla was being so patient with him. Steve felt better, knowing he had a 5-year-old parent looking out for him. The waves rolled in gently and whispered further reassurance. The sun was out now and bathed them in the warm 40-degree heat. They sat for a while longer. It was head clearing and soul cleansing. Steve sighed and breathed out. Breathed in. Breathed out. Like they taught him in meditation class. It felt good. Real good. He was going to make it. They all were. In their own way.

The End

Epilog Looking Back -How we made through Covid. (Sort of)

Looking back at the Pandemic (at least I hope we are for the most part), I'm not sure what, if anything, we learned.

Sometimes, it felt like we were the lucky ones who survived the Plague. Other times, it felt like we were all suffering from a global collective PTSD (i.e., Post Traumatic Stress Disorder.) Even now, the memories of that time are like a slow-motion blur that we don't know how to remember. Almost a form of collective amnesia. It was hard to live through. Even harder to explain. But that's what I wanted to do in this book for future readers trying to look back and understand it all or a part of it.

Certainly, there were grievous losses that continue to make our hearts heavy. People lost their spouses, partners, parents, siblings, children, friends with little or no warning. One day the departed were alive and vital, the next they were dead or attached to a breathing tube and we couldn't even visit them.

Heartbreaking. Others lost their health permanently (Continuing Long Term Covid), their homes, jobs and joy of spirit.

Covid is still out there, lurking. That's why it is still important to take reasonable precautions for yourself and others against Covid in confined spaces. Don't be embarrassed to be the one to wear a mask on a plane. When in doubt, get tested or self-quarantine for the sake of others. This is how you protect the ones you love.

As I sit here at 3:13 a.m. writing this ending, it is difficult to make sense of it all. Maybe we just can't. In researching this semi-autobiographical novel, I found it helpful, to read more knowledgeable authors on Covid. Two books I would recommend are: Word War C by Dr. Sanjay Gupta and The Plague Year by Lawrence Wright.

For me personally, what got me through these Hellish Years were 5 basic things:

1. Love from/to my family. (Especially Barbie, a true-life partner, editor and soulmate.)

2. Friends who kept me going and laughing. A cup of coffee or walk with friends is a lot cheaper and more meaningful than seeing a therapist. (Plus, there is still the advantage of no co-pay! And unlike a dog, there isn't any cleanup. Usually.) Thanks, Minneapolis and Chicago Coffee Clubs. You know who you are. Certainly, I can't forget the caring neighbors of our Chicago coop. Finally, all our friends in Chicago, Minneapolis and Arizona. The older I get, the more I realize that true wealth is having stalwart friends and an incredible lifetime partner. Sorry though, the Boss says you have to pay retail for the book this time. As a writer, you can never have too many friends when it comes to buying books.

3. Paying reasonable attention to my health and that of loved ones and friends. (Even the annoying ones.) I have taken simple steps like diet, exercise, rest and stress reduction. Shoulda, coulda done it sooner. For you, there may be other steps.

4. A positive outlook and good belly laugh. Remember hope is a great prescription for what ails you. Find optimism and

humor wherever you can. It's a rare gift to share with family and friends. (Thanks George, Michael, Marvin and Freada) Never take it for granted.

5. Luck or lack thereof. Accept it. Don't always have to understand it.

We all need to pay attention to our physical and mental health. (Some might add spiritual health.) After all, we only get this one physical and emotional body that we are currently inhabiting. Like a used car, we need to pay consistent, proper attention to our bodies. A lifetime warranty is still no guarantee against sudden mechanical breakdowns. Preventive maintenance is key. (My religious/spiritual friends tell me that's what prayer is for them: preventive and restorative maintenance. Sorry Barb, Rochel and Dovid, the jury is still out for me on that one.)

I need to thank my friends who were kind enough to endure several revisions of this and other novels including Rabbi Magal, Jerry (who donated valuable fly fishing time), Barb, Phil, Bettye, Larry (who knew an engineer could be such a good editor?) and of course Barbie who has encouraged and tolerated my creative meanderings over the years. Barb makes this journey called life more than worthwhile. Feel that touch, Barbie? That's me psychically squeezing your hand.

Most of all, I want to thank all of you who had the courage to keep moving forward even after the occasional fall. I know it isn't always easy. (See the Timeline that follows.) I'm especially thinking of all the young parents like my son, his coparent, my daughters, sons-in-law and their children who have shown admirable grace, courage and flexibility in meeting the challenges of the day. Hope there comes a time when they can finally catch their breath.

For the future generations, (Including our currently nonexistent great grandchildren- what can I say? Barb is very optimistic.) They will all face their own set of unique challenges.

But somehow, someway they will find their own path- even though they may falter along the way. We all trip and fall or get temporarily lost. (The latter seems to be a more common issue for directionally challenged males. Trust me, Barbie and I have learned this the hard way.) So, remember not to be discouraged by how many times you may fall on your life journey, you can still pick yourself up.

In any case, this book is for you.

Phil Finkelstein Author, June 2023

Timeline-The Lost Years or The Years That Weren't.

1. November 2002. SARS Disease kills almost 10% of those infected. Preview of coming pandemic.
2. December 30, 2019. Something wrong in Wuhan China. Dr Li who found it, later dies of Covid.
3. January 18, 2020. Chinese New Year. Many people in China travel to visit family.
4. January 20,2020. Total lockdown declared in Wuhan, a city of 11,000,000 people.
5. January 23,2020. U.S. Travel Ban to/from China.
6. January 29,2020. Coronavirus (Covid) Task Force established.
7. January 31,2020. HHS Secretary Azar announces Public Health Crisis.
8. February 3, 2020. U.S. declares Public Health Emergency.
9. February 11, 2020. World Health Organization names the virus: Covid 19.
10. February 20, 2020. President Trump announces: "One day like a miracle, it's gonna be gone."
11. March 11, 2020. World Health Organization declares Covid 19 a Pandemic.
12. March 13,2020. President Trump declares a Nationwide Emergency.
13. March 14, 2020. C.D.C. issues a No Sail Order to the cruise lines.
14. March 15, 2020. States, Cities, and Schools begin to shut down.
15. March 17, 2020. Moderna starts first human trial of Covid Vaccine.
16. March 26, 2020. U.S. Senate passes 2 Trillion Dollar Covid Relief Bill.
17. March 28,2020. White House extends social distancing rules.
18. April 13, 2020. President Trump announces the U.S. won't fund the World Health Organization.
19. April 23, 2020. President Trump suggests a powerful light or disinfectants may cure Covid.
20. April 30, 2020. President Trump announces Operation Warp Speed to make a vaccine.
21. May 9, 2020. Unemployment at 14.7%, the highest since Great Depression in the 1930's.
22. April/May 2020. States, Cities, Schools reopening with varying rules on masks + seating capacity.
23. May 25,2020. George Floyd dies in Minneapolis, Minnesota.
24. May 26, 2020. Large peaceful protests Floyd's death begin. Riots in a few cities including Mpls.
25. May 28, 2020. U.S. Covid deaths exceed 100,000.
26. June 1, 2020. Walk to Lafayette Park by President Trump after clearing protesters.
27. July 27, 2020. Moderna Vaccine begins Phase 3 trial.
28. November 3rd, 2020. Joe Biden elected President. President Trump refuses to accept results.
29. December 11, 2020. FDA approves Pfizer Covid Vaccine. Moderna approval is January 31. 2021.
30. January 6, 2021. Capital Riot and Occupation.
31. January 20, 2021. Inauguration of President Biden.
32. February 1, 2021. More Americans vaccinated than not.
33. February 22, 2021. U.S. Covid deaths exceed 300,000.
34. May 17, 2021. U.S. Covid deaths exceed 1,000,000.

Made in the USA
Monee, IL
28 August 2023

41747956R00134